NXT

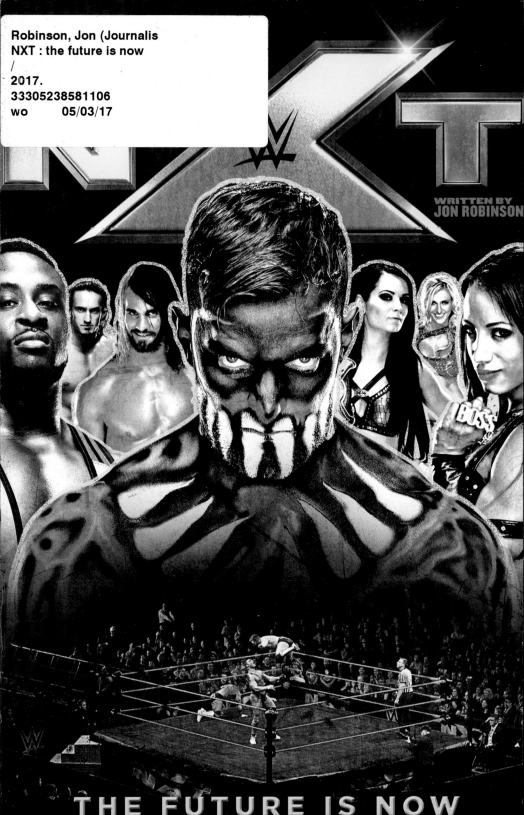

NXT

WRITTEN BY
JON ROBINSON

THE FUTURE IS NOW

Published by ECW Press
665 Gerrard Street East
Toronto, ON M4M 1Y2
416-694-3348 / info@ecwpress.com

Library and Archives Canada Cataloguing in Publication

Robinson, Jon (Journalist), author
NXT : the future is now / Jon Robinson ; foreword by Vincent K. McMahon.

Issued in print and electronic formats.
ISBN 978-1-77041-325-2 (hardback); ISBN 978-1-77090-979-3 (pdf); ISBN 978-1-77090-978-6 (epub)

1. WWE NXT (Television program). 2. Wrestling matches. 3. Wrestling. 4. Television broadcasting of sports.
I. McMahon, Vince, writer of foreword II. Title.

GV1196.25.R635 2017   796.812   C2016-906366-6
                             C2016-906367-4

Editor for the press: Michael Holmes
Cover design: Adam McGinnis
Type: Rachel Ironstone

Printing: Friesens   5   4   3   2   1

Printed and bound in Canada

TABLE OF
CONTENTS

Vincent K. McMahon

When my son-in-law Paul Levesque first described his dream to culti-vate the Superstars of tomorrow, even I could not imagine the revolu-tion that lay ahead. The NXT brand that started as a grassroots training ground has far surpassed its role and has become a movement among WWE fans around the world.

Within just a few short years, the WWE Universe has witnessed the creation of an epicenter for innovation—the WWE Performance Cen-ter—and within its walls, the development of a brilliant future. There, NXT has bred some of the most impressive competitors and matches of this era. It has attracted world-class talent from every stretch of the globe. It has also forged a strong bond with Full Sail University and its students, providing an opportunity to develop not only our performers, but also the next wave of producers and professionals—a community.

For a glimpse into this transformation, look no further than the many successful stars of today—many of whom have graduated from their days as NXT's remarkable athletes to become celebrated champi-ons on WWE's roster of globally recognized Superstars.

Kevin Owens. Seth Rollins. Bray Wyatt. Paige. Charlotte. Sasha Banks. The tremendous growth and progress made in Orlando can be easily measured by the accolades of these diverse and talented com-petitors, and so many others. NXT alumni have competed on "The Grandest Stage of Them All" at *WrestleMania*, inspired a Divas Revolu-tion, and carried our richest prize, the WWE Championship. NXT has produced this generation of WWE's greatest Superstars and beyond.

When Paul chose his destiny outside the ring in WWE, I knew to expect great things. I believed in his mission the day the doors first opened at the Performance Center and the night a new NXT debuted. Today, I watch in admiration of Paul's commitment to this most imperative initiative to shape our future. And I look forward to seeing this groundbreaking division flourish for many decades to come.

PART ONE

If You Build It,
They Will Come

CHAPTER 1
Game Changer

"The wrestling business is going to die unless we change our development system."

Those were the words of Paul "Triple H" Levesque as he sat down with WWE majority owner, chairman, and CEO, Vince McMahon, back in 2010. Triple H's full-time in-ring career was winding down, and McMahon wanted his son-in-law to begin his transition to office work. To do that, McMahon sent Levesque on a weekend retreat with the head of each department within WWE corporate. Over the course of two days, Levesque heard every last detail of the business outside of the ring, from marketing and public relations to retail and television production.

"The one thing that I thought was strange," says Levesque, "is that nobody was talking about where the future WWE Superstars would come from. I remember at the end of the meeting, Vince asked for everyone's takeaways. He wanted to know what we thought about the company and where it was headed. A couple people talked, and then Vince turned to me and asked, 'So, Paul, what do you think?' I hesitated at first because I didn't know I was going to be asked a question, but I said, 'Hey, I'm looking at all these things we're doing as a company and they're huge; they're awesome. As a performer, I had no idea about all the behind-the-scenes dealings that are going on as a global corporation, but I have yet to hear anybody say anything about what we're doing to create talent.'"

With WCW and ECW out of business, and territories a thing of the past, the days of signing top athletes from rival promotions were long gone, and Levesque feared that the talent pool of future Superstars would eventually disappear.

"Where will the talent come from?" Levesque asked the room of execs. And while he received nods of agreement from those around him, nobody else in the room stepped up to speak out about the issue, and the meeting quickly moved on to other matters. A couple of days later, however, Vince summoned Levesque into his office for a follow-up discussion.

"We need to create a new system," Levesque told McMahon. "We're a victim of our own success. We survived every other place closing their doors because you created a brand so successful that's all anyone will pay to see. But fast forward 20 years. Who are the nobodies today who will be somebodies tomorrow? I don't see anybody."

And while Vince was moved by Levesque's passion, once again, the matter went unresolved. In fact, it wasn't until 2012, when Levesque started to work full-time in the WWE office, that he was finally given the keys to development.

"When I started working at WWE Headquarters on a full-time basis, Vince told me to talk to everyone in the office and go through everything. He wanted me to find out what I was interested in. He gave me a ton of options for projects to work on, but I just came right back to development," says Levesque. "I told Vince, 'I'm back to where I was a couple of years ago. Everything in the company is fascinating, but where are we going to get our talent from? Where is our future headed without new talent?'"

At the time, WWE's development system was Florida Championship Wrestling, a small promotion run out of Tampa, housed in a tiny warehouse that was anything but big league, with live shows that typically ran in front of less than 20 people, and a television program that was broadcast only on local Florida TV.

"There was a huge disconnect with what we were doing at FCW and what was expected of talent once they made it to *Raw*," says Levesque.

"How can we expect someone to jump from working in front of a crowd of 40 and two cameras to a show at Madison Square Garden . . . and it's on live TV? Where are the cameras? What am I doing?"

"FCW TV didn't give you a lot to be excited about," adds Corey Graves, the NXT and *Raw* announcer who began his WWE training as an in-ring competitor in Tampa. "The matches were fine, but as far as production quality, it aired on some local Florida channel that all of 13 people got, and it just didn't feel like TV. There was no sense of accomplishment from being on FCW TV; it was just for practice. Back in those days, there was such a disconnect between the main office and FCW that the main roster and the office was like this mythical being. We knew they existed, but they didn't pay any attention to us. We were kind of this dirty little secret down in Tampa, doing what we wanted to do because no one was paying attention anyway.

"I remember people would come down from the office, whether it be a writer or someone from creative or a producer, and a swarm of guys would crawl over each other just to get a shot at talking to them. All anyone thought about was, 'Get me out of FCW! Put me on the main roster.' We just wanted to get on the road. We were tired of that warehouse, and it was like a dogfight to get ahead—to get attention. It wasn't even necessarily to get out of there, you just wanted to know that what you were doing was being paid attention to. Even if the only feedback you got was, 'Everything you're doing is wrong. You suck.' At least you knew that someone at WWE Headquarters realized you existed."

Beyond local Florida television, FCW talent were also being introduced to a national audience at the same time, thanks to *NXT* on SYFY, an experimental reality show that began in 2010. Unfortunately, at that time the show degraded the talent more than it showcased them, as each rookie was paired with a WWE veteran and was often made to look like a fool rather than the future of the business.

"When *NXT* originated, they said it was a reality show, but it was more like torture," says Bray Wyatt, who was featured on season two of *NXT* under the name Husky Harris. "When we were put on the

"Who are the nobodies today who will be somebodies tomorrow?"

original *NXT*, I remember William Regal walking up to us and saying, 'Fellas, I don't know how you do this. If this was how I started, I never would've made it.' Those weren't very encouraging words, but that's how the format was. We were thrust out there; we were nothing; we were embarrassed on a weekly basis, and we were given these horrible names with no creativity and nothing behind them. It kind of ruined us. It ruined all of us for a long time. It was a bad time, especially for me. I never felt like myself."

"I'm not necessarily sure it was designed to make stars," says Daniel Bryan. "Now that I saw what took place during the filming of *Tough Enough*, a show where new talent attempted to earn a contract through a reality TV setting, I realized that the most important part of the experience was to try to create a compelling TV show. That's why we were doing things like monkey bar climbs and drinking soda on not-quite live but nearly live TV. For someone who doesn't drink carbonation—it's like literally a million people watched me struggle to drink soda on live TV.

"I almost feel like being on *NXT* hurt me. The only positive was that by being paired up with The Miz and by being forced to lose every match, I gained a lot of sympathy, just because they treated me so poorly. I remember when I first went out and lost to Chris Jericho, it was no big deal; it was great for me to be in the ring with a legend like that and to be competitive. Then I lost the next week because of injuries; again, it's no big deal, it fits with the storyline. But then it became this thing where instead of losing for a good reason—to make me an underdog—it's like, 'Nope, he's just on a losing streak; he loses every match.' And because it's a short show—it's only an hour—and we have all these stupid competitions, I never had time to gain back any momentum. It was like, 'Hey, he's losing to these other rookies in two minutes because he's not very good.' What helped me was Michael Cole and those other guys burying me on commentary, saying, 'Oh, look at him, he's just a nerd.' And being paired with The Miz, who was legitimately not liked by the WWE Universe. So they were like, 'Hey, Miz is being mean to this guy, and we don't like Miz, so we are going to cheer for him

Kaitlyn participates in an NXT Rookie Divas Challenge: Last Sumo Standing.

Curtis Axel (then Michael McGillicutty) in the NXT Rookie Challenge: Power of the Punch.

even though he loses every match. And we hear these other guys talking about how bad he is, so we are going to cheer for him even more.' It just didn't seem like it was a good way to introduce stars."

Levesque agreed, and in 2012, when he was put in charge of the newly formed part of the company called Talent Development, it was up to him to change the culture.

Vince's words to Levesque were simple and to the point: "You told me what the problems were in development, now it's up to you to tell me how to fix it."

"My first goal was to create a bridge between the office and how we worked with talent," says Levesque. "That slowly morphed into something where I needed to take over talent relations and I needed to take over all of these other responsibilities in order to get it right."

Levesque headed to Tampa to take a closer look at what was really going on in FCW, and, more importantly, to figure out how to fix it. FCW live shows at the time were averaging 15 fans per date; there was more talent in the building than actual paying customers.

"When I was in FCW, it was very different. It was very much like an island unto its own," says Tyler Breeze, who began his WWE training under the name Mike Dalton in FCW. "Every now and then, they would have a showcase where Triple H or Undertaker or one of the writers would come down, and they would get to see everybody who was in FCW and what they were all about. It would give them a peek at who was down there. But that was only once every couple of months, maybe, so they didn't really keep up with the program, and it definitely wasn't a day-to-day type of thing."

Seth Rollins also saw the FCW process as extremely frustrating. "The brass didn't have eyes on us at all times. I think there was one guy in the office in Connecticut who was watching our tapes, and if he could get through to the brass in Connecticut, maybe we'd get a shot," says Rollins. "Otherwise, it was just what they needed at the time. Maybe they needed a Spanish-speaking guy; boink, let's pull him out. It's not like they were building prospects down in FCW. You just had to bite your tongue and deal with the taste of blood. It was a very difficult struggle for me, sitting there thinking I had so much to contribute and not being able to showcase that on a regular basis. The only way to temper that frustration is to dive into what you're doing."

Beyond fighting for the attention of the main office, another problem with FCW was the facility itself. A dingy warehouse with three rings and no gym, talent would arrive in the morning to work out in the ring, leave to lift weights at a local gym and eat, then return later in the day if they had a promo class to work on their mic skills with WWE Hall of Famer Dusty Rhodes.

"When I got to FCW, it was very different," explains Baron Corbin, who retired from the NFL to give his dream of sports entertainment a shot. "In FCW, we had street teams who postered towns with the shows. I was humbled greatly when I was given a sign and told to stand on the corner in town for hours, telling people to come to that night's show. 'Come to FCW, where you'll see the future stars of WWE.' Coming from the NFL, I was used to being treated well, and I came from an environment where everything was taken care of. When you're in the NFL, everybody bends over backwards for you; then you come here and you're standing on a street corner with a sign. It was really good for me. It was a humbling experience. In that locker room, all you had was a bathroom to change in and chairs along the wall. It was a grind. By no means was FCW easy."

Levesque talked to the talent and coaching staff of FCW, dug down deep into their development process, and walked away unimpressed. Even worse, he found the facility uninspired. While the coaching staff taught students wrestling basics, there was nothing at FCW that felt "next level" to Levesque, and the old-school training techniques of slamming bodies on mats to prove toughness just didn't jive with what modern athletes needed to transform into Superstars. And since FCW live events often featured more wrestlers than fans, students who were called up from development frequently found themselves overwhelmed at the differences between gym practice and *Raw* reality.

"I traveled down to Florida to visit FCW and see what they were doing, but they really weren't doing anything special. Then it was up to me to figure out how to change the process that talent went through so they could sign and train and be ready to step up and join the main roster," says Levesque. "We needed to create a system to design WWE Superstars. Knowing everything that I knew about being a WWE Superstar and knowing what I did in order to get there, I wanted to design a process that would help signed talent become Superstars who could carry the brand for the next decade.

"I thought, 'If I was a young kid who wanted to be a WWE Superstar, what would I need to do? How could I get there?' To me, it came down to a couple of things: we needed a first-class facility to attract the top talent from across the world. There are millions of people out there who are like, 'I'd love to become a WWE Superstar,' but that's like saying, 'I want to be a trapeze artist.' How do you even go about getting started? And how do you find the millions of people who want to do this? How do you attract them? It's one thing to say you want to

NXT Rookie Diva Jamie in a bull-riding competition.

do this; it's another thing to say, that you want to go to some dumpy warehouse in Florida with an audience of five people. How do you create a facility to attract them? How do you go about creating and giving talent a platform to do what they do best?

"When I went to WCW back in 1994, I didn't know anything about television. I learned it on the fly because I knew I needed to know it and nobody was teaching it to me. I just talked to everybody who was there and I learned what they did and how they did it and why it mattered. When I got to WWE, I had some knowledge of how television worked. If I didn't have that knowledge, there's no way I would've made it. So to me, new talent needs a smaller platform, so we can explain, 'Here's how you do it.' That way, when they get to the bigger platform and we tell them, 'Look at the hard camera,' they know what we're talking about. If you take a step beyond just the performers in the ring, I also realized that there needed to be a change on every level.

AJ Lee does the limbo during her time on the original *NXT*.

We had cameramen and technicians and directors and producers and all these people that, while they are great at what they do, they've been doing this for us for quite a while and are getting older. What if they decide they don't want to do this anymore? What do we do?

"We had to start over from square one and teach people on every level how we do what we do. And that was cameramen, technicians, ring announcers, commentators, play-by-play, all of it. I realized right then and there that we needed to change the game. We needed a new way to develop talent on all levels. The process started then."

But as Levesque's process began, rumors about FCW's demise started swirling out of control.

"A rumor broke on the internet one night; it was a Monday after *Raw*. Something had leaked out that FCW was out of business," says Graves. "There was a frenzy of texts between all of the boys and the coaches. We were all like, 'Did we just get fired?' I thought I had been fired over the internet. They just shut down FCW, so we didn't know what was going on. You learn to not believe everything you read on the internet, but when it's something like that, when it's something major like that, I really thought I had just been fired. I didn't know what to believe."

Levesque quickly squashed the rumor publicly, explaining that WWE Development was being revamped, not shut down. In the meantime, he was scouting locations for what he hoped would become his dream building: the WWE Performance Center.

"I had the idea for the facility; I had the concept for what I wanted to do; I just didn't know exactly what it was," says Levesque. "I knew what I needed to make, but I just didn't know the process of how to build it. So I went out and started looking at facilities. When WWE was in Pittsburgh, I went out to see what the Penguins facility looked like. I would be on the road and I would see some of these training facilities, and, honestly, I'd shrug my shoulders—I expected more. But then I did a photo shoot for a book at the Seattle Seahawks training center, and I was told at the time that they had one of the premiere facilities in the country, and that stuck in my mind. Then I went to MetLife and the

Timex Performance Center in New Jersey when we did the site survey for *WrestleMania*, and I was able to visit the New York Giants training facility, and I left there thinking that was exactly the type of place we needed. It was the nicest facility we had seen. It was just awesome. I left there and I was like, 'I'm making that.' All I had to do was convince someone to pay for it. I had to go back and talk to Vince and try to convince him to give me a couple million dollars. Nothing like this had ever existed, so it was a tough sell. It's not like you're the Giants and you need to build a football field to practice on. I had to back up and break down all of the equipment we would need and all of the things we would do. What do you need to be a WWE Superstar? What do I need to put in the building to facilitate these things? I had to think about the facility size, the layout, the number of rings. Then, after we opened, I came up with the padded crash ring where high-flying students could practice falling on the mat and diving from the top rope in a safe environment without fear of injury. The ring was built with a specially designed crash pad that features a foot of thickness to help absorb the energy of falling bodies. It's a process that helps students take steps forward in development while getting used to performing riskier moves thanks to the added padding. From there, we also added the green-screen room and the mirror room where people go to cut their own promos.

"We used to practice cutting promos in the backstage mirror or in our cars, but we needed to bring the business into the next generation of technology where talent can cut promos in front of a camera and watch it back immediately on an iPad. We needed to take development in an entirely new direction, but it's not cheap to do that. We needed to figure out how to do all those things, and then convince Vince to pay for them. It's not like we had a template to go on. This is something nobody had ever done before, and we knew we had to get it right. If you played high-level high school ball, if you played college, if you played pro for even one season, and then you decided you wanted to come to WWE—you're willing to take the gamble on the money and you're willing to take the gamble on the travel—would you be willing to go to this building every single day? You need to work your ass off because this isn't an easy profession, but if this facility is awesome, if this facility gives you everything you need as an athlete, you're more willing to make this leap. When you went to college as an athlete, college was awesome. You made no money, you were starving, but you loved training, you loved your teammates, and you had the time of your life because you were able to be an athlete.

"We wanted to recreate that experience. Build a facility where they think, 'I'll stay at this place all day. I'll come in the morning, I'll stay and eat lunch, I'll train here, I'll rehab here, it's awesome. Then I go do my shows and I come back and do it all over again. I'm getting paid to come to this kick-ass multi-million-dollar facility and become the best athlete I can be.' If they have that, all that other stuff doesn't matter to a 22-year-old kid who is just trying to be an athlete.

"That's what we needed to build."

Matt Striker hosts another Rookie Challenge on *NXT* season two.

CHAPTER 2
Welcome to Orlando

As Paul Levesque continued to scout locations for his new development center, his focus remained on the state of Florida. Not only do a lot of current and former WWE Superstars call the state home, but the elimination of state tax (saving talent thousands of dollars per year) and the pleasant weather made Florida preferential to employees.

"Florida has had this rich history of wrestling, going back to when Dusty Rhodes ran the territory," says NXT Superstar Samoa Joe. "It was dormant for a long time, and from speaking to people within WWE, for a while, Orlando was a city that they would designate as not really a hot spot or someplace that drew well. But Florida is a wrestling state. The people have always loved wrestling, it just needed a new brand to revitalize the area and spark that interest."

"I can say, 'You want to come to Stamford, Connecticut?' and listen as they talk about how cold it gets up there and the snow, or I can say, 'Do you want to come to Orlando, with the theme parks, fun nightlife, and great weather all year round?'" says Levesque. "It's a resort destination. So it's very attractive. I was heavily looking at locations in Florida all along, but I hadn't made my final decision until I stumbled into Full Sail University."

Levesque had heard about the Orlando-based college, a school focused on training students in careers in media arts, entertainment and technology, and was intrigued. It just so happened, *Raw* was scheduled to broadcast live out of Orlando at that time, so Levesque was already in the area. He took advantage of the timing to set up a campus tour, hoping to find out more about the classes they offered and how they trained people to learn television production in their massive facility that housed over 100 studios on-site.

"When I showed up, they were ready to give me a tour. I was looking at this one building they had, and they asked, 'Why are you so interested in that building?' And I was like, 'Because I can shoot a TV show out of here.' Everyone asked, 'What TV show?' And I said, 'I have an idea for a wrestling show.' We all went upstairs and I asked them, 'What would it take for me to shoot a TV show out of here?' And they told me to come back and give it a try, shoot a pilot, and see

Triple H's press conference with Florida Governor Rick Scott during the ceremonial groundbreaking of the WWE Performance Center.

View from the front of house at Full Sail Live.

how it worked out. They said they wouldn't charge me anything, and that the students would help run the show. So I came in and shot the pilot, and it turned out better than anyone thought. That became the deciding factor of where the Performance Center would be. I knew if I was going to shoot the television show at Full Sail, the facility would have to be close."

On May 17, 2012, the first four episodes of Levesque's secret project were taped at Full Sail University, in a show where not even the talent knew exactly what was going on. The branding ringside and throughout the building was NXT, but this was anything but a reboot of the reality TV show. The NXT viewers had soured on was about to be wiped from existence and replaced with a show that would spark a revolution.

"We were kept in the dark," says Graves. "All we knew was that we had this special taping at Full Sail University; beyond that, we really

> **"I could see the foundation of something that could be really cool."**

weren't given many details. We thought it was just a one-off deal. I remember Dusty was really excited about it, and he told us all it was a big deal, but he wouldn't tell us why. So we went there, and there was a handful of matches, but nothing was really revealed to us. I remember when I got there, I saw the set and was like, 'Wow, this is pretty big time compared to our little FCW TV,' which was shot at some warehouse in Tampa. We got there and all the branding on the ring was NXT, so that's the first time we even got a hint that what we were doing was going to be known as NXT. But nothing was officially told to us. I remember we did those tapings, and then nothing happened for a while. We didn't know what was going on. But we were all like, 'That was great, wouldn't it be amazing if we could do the show there all the time?' That ended up being the pilot episode, and, luckily, enough people liked what we were doing that we were able to go back and make it our regular spot."

Levesque adds, "Once we shot the first few episodes at Full Sail and I could see that this was becoming a reality, so I started looking at more and more locations around Orlando, but Full Sail was the key to everything. I needed a place to teach camera guys, I needed to teach referees, I needed to teach ring announcers, I needed to teach play-by-play guys.

Paul "Triple H" Levesque presents his vision for the future of talent development.

We had our team on the main roster, but we didn't have any back-up, and when I was looking around at our team, I realized, man, this camera guy has been here for 15 years. How long is he going to want to be a camera guy for us, another 10? Then what? We shoot things a particular way, and that's why we use the same people all the time. We don't like when people come from other places because they don't do what we do, they do a different version of it. Right or wrong, it's just not exactly what we do, so we need to retrain them. We need to have people ready to roll as we move into the future, and Full Sail enables me to train everyone from the athletes in the ring to the cameramen capturing the footage to the announcers calling the action. Thanks to Full Sail, I had now narrowed my search to Orlando, and after the first set of tapings, we were even more focused."

And while Levesque admits that the first tapings weren't perfect, they were more than enough to help him focus his vision.

"Coming here and shooting the pilot was nerve-wracking, but when it was done and I watched the final content—yeah there were holes in it, and yeah it wasn't phenomenal—I could see the foundation of something that could be really cool," says Levesque. "I showed that to Vince and I gave my best sales pitch at doing more with it, and he bought into that."

McMahon agreed to take the *NXT* reality show off the air, re-branding development as NXT and moving forward with Levesque's new concept. "I had the talent, I had the stars, but that buy-in from Vince that said, 'Yeah, we can do this,' was a huge turning point," says Levesque. "The first couple of shows we did were rough. The talent were rough. The shooting was rough. It was a lot of creative editing, but you could see the template of something there."

On June 19, 2012, WWE announced that Levesque's new *NXT* program would air exclusively on Hulu and Hulu Plus in the United States, while also being broadcast internationally thanks to deals already in place through the *NXT* reality series. The first few episodes of the new-look show featured the likes of Seth Rollins, The Ascension, Bo Dallas, Cesaro, The Usos, Paige, and Bray Wyatt. On August 1, newly appointed NXT Commissioner Dusty Rhodes announced a Gold Rush Tournament to decide the first official NXT Champion, as all FCW titles were being deactivated.

NXT was now officially the brand name of WWE development, and NXT needed a champion to call its own.

The Gold Rush Tournament featured eight competitors, four current NXT stars and four stars from WWE's main roster. Opening-round matches included Richie Steamboat versus Leo Kruger, Jinder Mahal versus Bo Dallas, Seth Rollins versus Drew McIntyre, and Michael McGillicutty versus Justin Gabriel.

In the tournament finals, Seth Rollins pinned Mahal to win and become NXT's first Champion.

"It's really special to be known as the first NXT Champion, but back when I won, we were still training out of the FCW warehouse, and

Seth Rollins defeats Jinder Mahal on August 29, 2012, to become the inaugural NXT Champion. Triple H and Dusty Rhodes congratulate him in the ring.

every day was a grind," says Rollins. "It was a grimy little warehouse. It wasn't spectacular. We didn't have this cult following. We didn't have people waiting outside trying to get our autographs, we didn't have a show on WWE Network or anything like that."

But eight months later, everything changed when Levesque finally chose a non-descript Orlando office park to house his Performance Center.

"It was just whispers. Everybody heard whispers. It was never confirmed. And then it was like, 'Hey, we have this building, this is happening,'" says Corbin. "Still, even then, you're like, 'Okay, I'll believe it when I see it.'"

On April 18, 2013, WWE broke ground in suburban Orlando (just a few minutes away from Full Sail), showing the designs of their 26,000-square-foot building to the public for the first time, and on July

WWE breaks ground on its Performance Center on April 18, 2013.
Left to Right: Adrian Neville, Corey Graves, Mason Ryan,
Triple H, Connor O'Brien, Paige, Xavier Woods.

11, the multi-million dollar Performance Center was open for business. FCW was no more, with talent making the move from Tampa to Orlando to not only train, but also to continue to tape new episodes of *NXT* at Full Sail.

"I was making some trips up from Tampa to help move in, and you start to see everything come together, and it's eye-opening," says Corbin. "First day we started here, it was like, this is real. Everything we heard is true. This is happening. But when you first start to hear things, you doubt it, especially when you're in a little warehouse with a couple of rings and it's musty. They're telling you about how they hope to have seven rings, a weight room, and green screens, and you're like, 'Yeah right.'"

"I remember there was a handful of us who got to go to the groundbreaking when they first started construction on the place, and

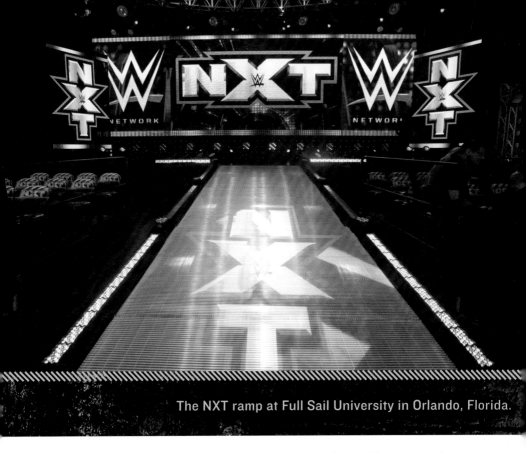

The NXT ramp at Full Sail University in Orlando, Florida.

I remember walking into the building and just being blown away by the size of everything," adds Graves. "They tell you the specs, but it's not until you actually walk in and see what they've done that it's like, 'Oh my God, this is real.'"

"It's cool because I think Floridians like having something regional," says Samoa Joe. "NXT, in a certain aspect, is something they can call their own. Orlando is a real cultural melting pot, and I think NXT really reflects that in a lot of ways. You have athletes from all over the world on our roster, and when you take a spin around Orlando, you see it's a super multicultural society. I think there is something there for everybody, and when you combine all of those factors, it has helped make NXT what it is today."

Paul Levesque's dream building was now constructed, but his plans for overhauling development were only beginning.

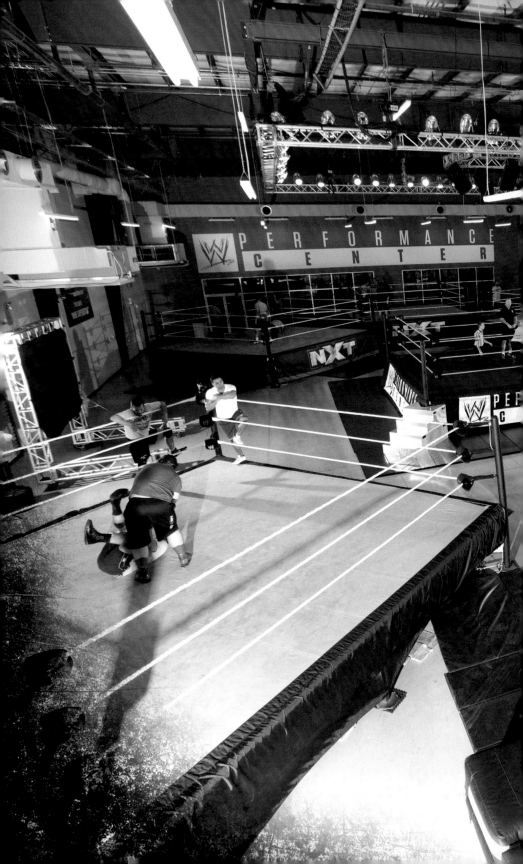

CHAPTER 3
And You Can't Teach That

Paul Levesque sits in his Performance Center office, phone vibrating every few seconds as both Vince and Stephanie McMahon attempt to reach him. The McMahons have a question about an upcoming ESPN segment featuring Brock Lesnar. As Levesque gives his advice on how to best handle the situation and ends his call, he quickly transitions back into talking NXT, explaining how the evolution of WWE's development program was sparked by a meeting with the former president of the NFL Player's Association, Nolan Harrison.

"When I got out of the NFL, I wanted to be a WWE Superstar," Harrison told him. "I just didn't know how to do it. I didn't know who to call and I asked everybody I could think of, and nobody really knew and nobody could think of anything. It just went by the wayside and I never did it."

"Those were the kinds of things I was trying to avoid," says Levesque. "There are athletes out there from all walks of life, be it the NFL, amateur wrestling, power lifting, whatever the case may be, and they'd like nothing more than to be a WWE Superstar—the biggest passion they have in life is WWE—but in the past, they just didn't know how to accomplish that goal. They didn't know how to fulfill that dream. But the Performance Center in Orlando gives us a facility where world-class athletes can come and test their skills and see if they have what it takes to be a WWE Superstar.

"We started to create this system that has a facility and has a program that entices people to want to be a part of it, not just say, 'Well,

Trainees work out inside the 5,500-square-foot WWE Performance Center gym.

Corey Graves inside the WWE Performance Center green-screen room.

you know, I could go do all this stuff on my own, but I don't know, it's a pipe dream.' This is a 'Here's how you do it and here's a place to do it in and it's a really cool thing to be a part of.' And on every level we're teaching the future of the business."

Inside the new WWE Performance Center sits seven full-sized rings, a 5,500-square-foot gym that includes everything from CrossFit to world-class weights and exercise equipment, high-tech video production and editing suites, hot and cold whirlpools, a full-time medical staff on-site five days a week, voice-over rooms for talent to learn play-by-play and color-commentary skills, a green-screen room to help create character video packages, and even Levesque's new high-tech mirror room where talent can not only practice promo skills in front of a camera, but also they can watch it back immediately on an iPad and get instant feedback from peers and coaches.

What might have been a half-day spent at FCW is now a full-time gig in NXT as the performers spend a majority of their day training for their opportunity to earn a spot on the main roster.

"We get down to the ring and are ready to stretch by 8:15 am," explains Bayley. "By 8:30, we're in the ring and we warm up and start going through routines. We have different themes of the month, like suplex month or submission month, and we work on those things. Then we have an hour break, and then we're in the gym for about an hour and a half to two hours with Matt Wichlinski, our strength coach. He has a workout plan for everybody, and if you have certain goals, he will change things accordingly. He'll even help us with our eating plans. And we have the best gym ever. It's CrossFit, power lifting, body building, and gymnastics all in one. There are huge tires, ropes . . . anything you need is in there. There's no excuse not to get in shape. Depending on the day, we also have promo class. So we can go home after the gym, then come back and cut promos. That's the toughest part of my day because I'm not great at promos. I really have to work hard in that class, but the only way to get better is to constantly practice. So we're here for six to seven hours depending on the day."

"It was an absolute shock to go from FCW to the Performance Center," says Sami Zayn. "Since the Performance Center opened, it has gradually added pieces and parts. And now when you step back and look at it, it's completely state of the art. It really is. I know everyone is always saying how great it is, but it really is a special building when it comes to training talent. My training was so bare bones and limited, so to see the access and the tools the talent has now—it's unbelievable.

"In my hometown of Montreal, my trainer was just a local guy who maybe wrestled for a year. I don't think he even finished training himself, to be honest, and I was learning to take bumps on the grass. But his philosophy was once you learn to fall on grass, a ring will be

Future WWE Women's Champion Sasha Banks trains with free weights.

easy. Which is true, but it's still probably better to train in a ring with actual security measures. I was just young and naive and wanted to get training any way I could, so I just took it. I'm still grateful because I'm here now, but my upbringing and my own training has really helped me appreciate what the Performance Center is and what it offers. If you walk in and this is your first experience, you might think a building like this is par for the course, but it isn't."

Neville mirrors Zayn's sentiments. "I started training when I was 18 years old on judo mats in a sports center. There were no rings. The gym was wherever you could find space. There wasn't anything like the Performance Center, so it was more like grassroots learning on the fly. If I had been able to come to the Performance Center early in my career, I think my development would have gone so much smoother, and who knows how much better off I'd be. It took me 10 years to reach WWE, but if I had the Performance Center when I started, I'm

The WWE Performance Center features seven rings as well as a ramp for rehearsing entrances.

sure I would have been on *Raw* a lot sooner.

"Triple H has built a development center that covers everything. Anything you could imagine, they're ready for."

To Big Cass, the Performance Center signifies a huge leap forward for NXT. It gives the training staff the opportunity to teach new talent the finer points of becoming a WWE Superstar. "Coming to the Performance Center was mind-blowing," he says. "We even have things like a crash-pad ring— its only purpose is to practice high rope moves." But it's not just the more secure bumps inside the seven rings that impressed Big Cass; the technology inside the building is like nothing he has ever experienced before. "Everything filmed in the green-screen room, all of our promos and pitches, can go directly to WWE Headquarters in Stamford. Then they can send back immediate feedback on what they like or don't like. We also have a mirror room, our confessional where we practice promos. And via a login system, we have access to everything that is filmed. We can watch our matches; we can watch any promo we've ever done. Everything you ever need is at your fingertips. You never even need to leave this building. If you pack your lunch, pack your breakfast, you don't ever have to leave the building. You have the gym to work out and a physical-therapy room that is state of the art. It's a one-stop shop of training."

And while the NXT talent were buzzing about the new Performance Center, their matches were slowly creating buzz on the internet, thanks to an exciting brand of fast-paced wrestling adopted from the independent scene. On August 24, 2013, indie darlings Antonio Cesaro and Sami

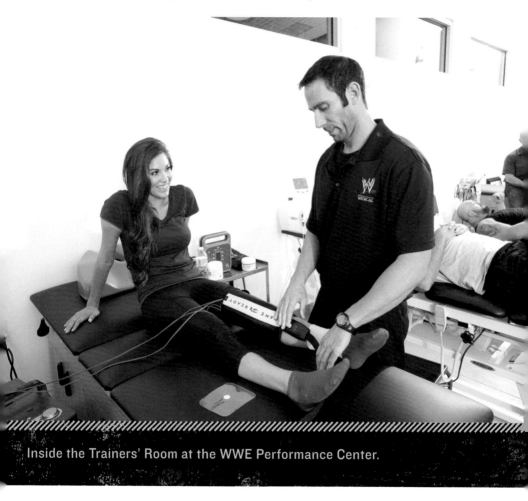

Inside the Trainers' Room at the WWE Performance Center.

Zayn squared off in a two-out-of-three-falls match that will forever go down as one of the top matches in NXT history, and it's a match that instantly became a hit across social-networking platforms like Twitter.

"Cesaro versus Sami Zayn; I think they were the catalyst to making this thing big," says Matt Bloom (aka Prince Albert, A-Train, Tensai and Sweet T), who currently works as the Head Coach at the WWE Performance Center. "That's when I started to notice. It might have started well before that, but I was commentating that match, and I had my headset on and I was watching the monitor, and Michael Cole came over like, 'Are you going to talk?' and I was like, 'Oh my God, I forgot I'm actually calling a match right now!' I was, and I still am, such a fan of what we produce that watching that match and hearing the buzz in the building just took me aback, and I knew big things were happening. Paul's really good at what he does, so for him to have the insight to see this whole image and what it should be and what it would become is incredible. I'm sure he thought it out well in advance and probably bounced it off a lot of intelligent people, so this was destined to do well. But Cesaro versus Sami Zayn, that's when I noticed just how special and just how big this could really be. That was the match that helped define what NXT would become."

In FCW, coaches attempted to squash the creativity of matches and moves in favor of making all talent work at a slower pace with more reined-in sets. The high spots and frenetic pace of the independent scene were frowned upon in Tampa, but in NXT, the talent were given more freedom, especially Superstars like Zayn and Cesaro, who were now able to capture what made them fan favorites on the indies and adapt that style under the new NXT banner.

"Cesaro's involvement was crucial in my development. It was that lightbulb moment for me on how to adapt my independent style to the WWE product," says Zayn. "They don't necessarily have to be night and day, but before that match, the mentality here was really different. The attitude here was a lot more like walking on eggshells, especially when it came to your in-ring performance. It was about conforming

Future WWE Women's Champion Charlotte Flair uses the rings in the WWE Performance Center gym.

"We're teaching the future of the business."

to a certain style and fitting inside a certain box. Working with Cesaro helped me see the WWE cameras and angles and what they're looking for from a performer and from a match. I was finally able to see how my style from my independent days could merge into the WWE world. Having Cesaro here was a perfect bridge for me. To get the chance to work with guys like Rhyno and Brian Kendrick, guys who have WWE experience, is invaluable. A lot of these students didn't have access to talent of this caliber on the independent circuit. Not everyone took the same route to get to the Performance Center, but for the guys who didn't get that experience, they're getting it now. These are big matches, big moments."

"NXT is essentially what Ring of Honor was in 2004 or ECW before that. It's an alternative to the WWE product; the major difference being WWE actually owns it," says Cesaro. "WWE realized that there is a market and obviously an audience for that style of wrestling, and they made their development system to capitalize on that. It was a smart business decision. NXT was around for a bit, but I feel my matches with Sami Zayn helped spark people's interests, and that made them realize that there was something special going on here. There were many other people doing special matches at the same time as well who helped with that movement, and the matches the NXT roster put on just kept getting better and better, pushing the brand further.

"Triple H was smart enough to realize that there's an audience out there who wants to watch the type of matches and the type of show *NXT* is. If you look at it this way, Vince McMahon took over the territory business, and now Triple H is taking over the indies. He just gave the WWE Universe an alternative, and it benefits both the NXT Superstars and WWE fans. It gives the NXT up-and-coming talent a platform to hone their craft while giving the hardcore fans an alternative to watch. It's definitely a win-win."

"NXT was slowly starting to pick up this kind of behind-the-scenes cult following, thanks to Zayn and Cesaro," says Levesque. "Most people were seeing it either on the internet on YouTube or catching little bits and pieces of it here and there. We were seen internationally; we didn't have a home domestically. We put it out on Hulu and we would put stuff up on YouTube. But the WWE Universe was catching on to it. They were slowly but surely spreading the word for us. It was starting to get a bit of a buzz around it and it was clear to me that people wanted more."

Bray Wyatt gives credit to Levesque for inspiring his Superstars-in-the-making with post-event pep talks that laid everything on the table, inspiring them to go all out on every show. "When Hunter and producer Michael Hayes would get up there and talk to us after the *NXT* tapings, it was not for the faint of heart," says Wyatt. "It was to weed out the cowards. 'Who wants it? Who is going to take it? Who is here just to collect a pay check and say that they did something that they never actually did?' Hunter would get in front of you and he would ride you, and he created this competitive atmosphere. That's been our MO ever since. We want it. It's ours, ours, ours! We're going to continue that. It's awesome.

"Hunter would challenge us. He would motivate us. One time, he showed us this Floyd Mayweather video where Floyd was holding his breath underwater, and it builds and builds and builds to this crescendo of 'nobody can hold us down.' That was the whole mentality there. You have to look at it from Hunter's perspective. No one knew what to expect at first; this was uncharted territory. He's taking a bunch of relative unknowns, putting us on a platform, and giving us a chance. It's something only Hunter can do. Hunter had faith in us, but he wasn't just going to let us slide and give us the world. He wanted us to earn it. He wanted us to take it. We would go out there like every night was *WrestleMania*.

"It was all stress, balls to the wall, whatever you got, and that was the mentality he gave us. Hunter challenged us: who is it going to be? I remember he took a group of us, the Wyatts, the Shield, and a couple of other guys who have since been called up, and he challenged us specifically. 'This is your house; what are you going to do with this?' He said, 'I can't make this happen, only you can,' and he put it on our shoulders. That's the great thing about Hunter, and it's the great thing about this business. When you're called upon, who can answer the bell?"

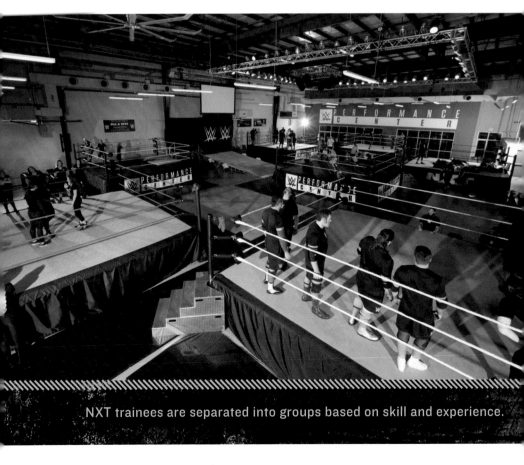

NXT trainees are separated into groups based on skill and experience.

CHAPTER 4
Arrival

As 2014 rolled around, plans for the WWE Network were finally beginning to take shape. The streaming network would air beginning February 24, 2014, complete with historic episodes of *Raw* and pay-per-views, but WWE was also looking for a way to test the service with live events. This was an entirely new business model for WWE, and if live events could help draw subscribers, it could lead to a unique way to present WWE to its Universe. With streaming services like Netflix and Hulu already stealing eyeballs away from traditional television, WWE didn't want to be left behind.

NXT was about to get its shot at the spotlight. Now it was up to the roster to step up and show the entertainment world what this new brand was all about.

"When the decision was made to go forward with the Network, there was an opportunity with *WrestleMania* coming up, but there were a lot of nerves. What if this doesn't work? So they wanted to test out the product," Paul Levesque says. "We were doing these little shows, but they were starting to get some social media buzz and the brand seemed to be picking up enough steam that I wondered if I could do an internet pay-per-view for $10 a whack. I wondered how many people would watch. We didn't know. We didn't get numbers. We didn't get ratings. I was just reading social media buzz. So the WWE Network launched, and I made a suggestion: how about we take my little development brand and shoot live at Full Sail. It's a test."

As Levesque saw things, if the live event failed and the Network

Triple H and Stephanie McMahon monitor the action from "Gorilla" position at Full Sail Live.

crashed, "NXT is the one who shits the bed the first week of the Network, not *WrestleMania,* which was only five weeks away."

But Levesque had faith in his crew to produce a quality live show; he knew he had the talent to create something special. "We had this dry run to see how it would do, just putting matches on Hulu and on YouTube, and it got so much buzz; people wanted more," says Levesque. "There were all these little moments along the way that helped lead up to this event, but I called that show *Arrival* because I felt like that was going to be our moment—this show was our arrival."

Levesque wanted to prove to McMahon and the WWE Universe that his roster was ready for the big stage.

"This show was our arrival."

"We'd done enough shows that I knew that as long as we stayed on the air and the satellite worked and the Network held up, we'd turn people's heads," says Levesque.

And turn heads it did. *NXT Arrival* aired on February 27, 2014, and it may have featured only six matches, but critics and fans alike saw an event truly unique in the WWE Universe at the time. A raucous sold-out crowd of 400 jammed inside Full Sail to witness NXT's Network debut that included Cesaro defeating Sami Zayn, Mojo Rawley defeating CJ Parker, The Ascension defeating Too Cool in a surprise return, Paige defeating Emma, Tyler Breeze and Xavier Woods fighting to a no contest, and Adrian Neville defeating Bo Dallas in a Ladder Match (the first in NXT's history) to become the new NXT Champion.

But while *Arrival* succeeded in putting on an action-packed show, the "test run" also had its share of headaches and glitches. Tickets for the event were oversold, leaving many fans outside the venue unable to watch the show live. In addition, the WWE Network feed cut out during the Breeze-Woods match, causing viewers to miss most of the highly anticipated battle. Still, even with its faults, *Arrival*'s captivating in-ring skirmishes warranted multiple re-watches among fans who loudly sang the praises of their new favorite show.

"To me, *Arrival* was the 'Earth isn't flat' moment," says Levesque. "It was the moment when people went, 'Whoa, what is this again?' The amount of people who watched it, more importantly the amount of social media buzz that it created the next day, was mind-blowing. Not that many people had the Network; people didn't even know what it was. But all of a sudden, the next day, everybody was talking about NXT."

Vince McMahon took notice of the overwhelming social media buzz, and talk turned from NXT as experiment to making its live shows quarterly events. "That move allowed us to plan for the future," explains Levesque. "Now that NXT was on the Network, it was starting to earn viewers and we were able to tell episodic stories and create a brand."

Levesque also saw each of the live shows as challenges unto themselves. He was out to prove that *Arrival* wasn't just a fluke. "Strate-

Rabid fans flock to Full Sail on February 27, 2014, for *NXT Arrival*.

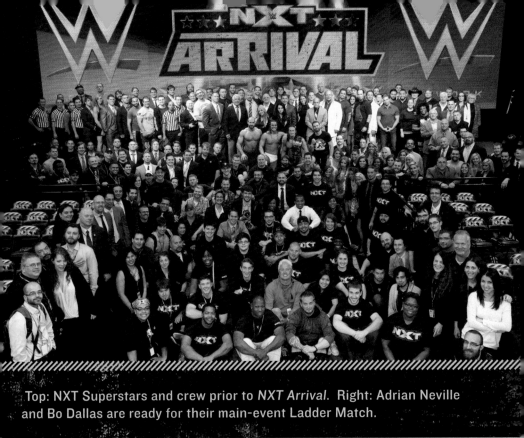

Top: NXT Superstars and crew prior to *NXT Arrival*. Right: Adrian Neville and Bo Dallas are ready for their main-event Ladder Match.

gically, each show was almost like a eureka moment in itself," says Levesque. "*Arrival* was exactly what we said it was: the arrival. When you went past that, it was almost like we could've called the next one 'It Wasn't a Fluke.' And then the next one would've been 'See? Told Ya.' Because everybody kept thinking, 'Yeah, it's the excitement of the initial one; yeah, they did two and that's cool, but they can't keep going.' But each show just kept getting bigger and better. Meanwhile, we were building this brand that had this cult following that was starting to become more and more recognizable. That's why we eventually wanted to name a show 'Takeover,' because we were taking over the WWE Network."

But it wasn't only those in attendance who were left impressed with NXT's arrival on the scene. *NXT Arrival* was so spectacular, a Superstar WWE had been trying to sign since 2010 decided to make NXT his new home.

Finn Bálor signed with WWE months after *NXT Arrival*.

"I'd been wrestling in Japan for years, and there had been an open line of communication between myself and WWE for a long time," says Finn Bálor. "We'd talked about the possibility of me coming to WWE, but back in 2010 and 2011, it just never felt like the right time. I wanted to tour Japan, as that landscape really suited me. But the first NXT special on WWE Network had this incredible buzz about it and a lot of my friends, like Sami Zayn and Adrian Neville, were already in NXT and they were all making an impact. I've always prided myself on having my finger on the pulse of what's cool and being in the right place at the right time, and I felt like NXT, and not Japan, was cool, so I wanted to be in NXT. I wanted to be a part of something, so when the opportunity came to make the switch to NXT, I joined. And I haven't looked back since.

"There were a lot of things on my mind about joining NXT, but when I talked to William Regal about it, he said that I needed to treat it like a new territory. He told me I needed to go in and work my way up from the bottom, and when he explained it in such simple terms, I agreed. NXT is the new territory, they need new talent, and I want to be one of those talents who comes in and works his way up from the bottom, just like I had done in Japan. It was a fresh challenge for me, it was something different, and it was the perfect stepping stone for me to adjust the styles I had been using in Japan to the hybrid NXT style. It really couldn't have been a better place for me to make my splash in the United States."

CHAPTER 5
All Eyes on Me

When the Performance Center opened, the plan was to have seven coaches oversee seven rings, with development talent graduating from one ring/coach to the next in order to learn all areas of wrestling expertise, from basic holds to submissions to top-rope maneuvers. At the same time, not only were the coaches and the NXT creative team watching from within the building, but Levesque actually had a camera inserted in the training room (it was quickly dubbed "Brother in the Sky") so that at any time throughout the day, there would be a live feed that he and Vince McMahon could watch while at WWE's corporate office in Stamford. More importantly, it was the exact opposite of the FCW experience, where talent were basically climbing over one another in order to get exposure. In NXT, everyone was put on notice: Big Brother is always watching. And as each live event seemed to one-up the previous show, and with *NXT* airing regularly on the WWE Network, the pressure was on the performers to step up their overall game.

"I tell people to work like their boss is watching all the time because in a real sense, he could be," says Terry Taylor, one of the coaches at the Performance Center. "We owe it to the people giving us our pay to give it our best effort. These guys are being paid to go to college, with a job waiting for them when they graduate. How could they not apply themselves? Sure, it's human nature to slack off now and again. Just don't do it in NXT."

Students learn quickly that NXT is not a place to simply "go through the motions." If they do, their career in WWE's ring will be short. Especially with a coaching staff who has done and seen it all. Levesque built a staff to educate the development talent in all aspects of the business, choosing coaches and advisors who he believed were the best of the best, including holdovers from FCW, Dusty Rhodes and Norman Smiley, while adding the likes of Matt Bloom, Billy Gunn, William Regal, Sara Amato and Adam Pearce so the development talent would have a higher coach-to-student ratio than anything seen in the old FCW days.

"In the old days, there were 28 territories nationally across the United States, plus Mexico, Australia, and Japan. Talent would spend three months to a year in as many of those places as they could to

Coach Terry Taylor with Mojo Rawley and Adam Rose.

hone their craft," says Taylor. "They'd learn how to perform in front of different crowds, and they'd learn what worked for them in front of those crowds and for themselves. They would then take what they had learned and move on to the next territory, getting better and better. It's refining your craft. It's like chipping away at a gem, and the more experience you gain, the more you chip away to reveal this perfect, polished stone. The gem is what their character is when they finally get into a bigger position, maybe eight to 10 years later. If you wanted to draw money, you needed to keep the crowds invested, and if you could draw crowds, promoters would pay you a lot of money to perform in their territory until your act grew stale, then you just took your character to the next place and did it all over again. That's how it used to be. Today there are no territories. So if the future of our business is based on fresh, young talent, where does it come from? The answer is the WWE Performance Center. From all walks of life, from all corners of the world, from every kind of occupation, our company goes out and seeks the best of the best and brings them here to teach them the art of what we do.

"The great thing about the WWE Performance Center and NXT is this: a comedian can tell jokes to a mirror and think he's funny, but until he gets that feedback from an audience, he never learns timing. We teach them the joke, the setup, the delivery, the timing, and the punchline. We teach them everything they need to know, then we put them in front of a live crowd at these *NXT* shows, and that's how they learn when to do things, how to deliver to a payoff, how to take everything they've learned here and apply it to something that works in front of a live crowd."

Levesque sees Taylor as a gifted trainer, not because of Taylor's days working WWE and WCW (even helping shape a young Levesque behind the scenes of WCW), but because of his ability to teach what it takes to be a true Superstar. To Levesque, in order to create the next John Cena, it's more important to have coaches who have the correct mentality in place than someone who has walked in Cena's main-event shoes.

"I used to have a very firm belief that in order to train people, you had to have been a top-level Superstar. If you've never been to the Super Bowl, how can you train people to get them to the Super Bowl?" asks Levesque. "That was my perception, but now, after going through it, I have a different opinion. There are trainers at all different levels, and there are trainers for all different skill sets. There are trainers who are great at footwork and the basics. There are trainers who are great at the intermediate stuff. There are trainers who are great at teaching you how to put together matches. But those trainers are few and far between, so you have to go out and find people who have these skill sets and work with them on how to teach others these skills. Then there are trainers like Terry Taylor, whose gift is teaching somebody how to be a star and how to be more than just technically good. Terry Taylor is a guy who, at a very formative time in my career in WCW, taught me a ton, so when I got to WWE, I had the tools to become a star. Terry taught me that—so I know it works. But if you look at Terry, you'd say, Terry was never in the main event of *WrestleMania*—and that's not a knock on his career. That's somehow become a knock on someone's career now; if they've never headlined *WrestleMania*, then they are lacking in their career, but that's just not the case. There is legend after legend after legend in this business who were mid-card guys, if you want to break it down in those terms. Terry was an unbelievably gifted performer. Arn Anderson talks about how people label him, and Arn will tell you, 'I was a mid-card guy. I never headlined anything unless I was tagging with Ric Flair.'

"So here's Arn Anderson, one of the biggest legends in this business, part of the Four Horsemen, and technically, he's right. He was in a tag team in WCW, he was in a tag team in WWE, and he never headlined individually. But in the ring and promo-wise, Arn Anderson is one of the best ever. You just need to step back and realize that there are people who were mid-card guys, but they understand how to teach, and they understand how to coach. At the same time, I've listened to some of the biggest stars try to train new talent, and I've started laughing, like, 'You actually have no idea how to do this, do you? You have no idea how you became a big star.' And some of them are my best friends. There are a lot of guys, like Ray 'The Crippler' Stevens, who historians will tell you was one of the greatest performers to ever step in the ring, but if you ask Ray how he did it or why he did a certain move at a certain time, he'd tell you, 'I don't know. I just did it.' He doesn't know. It was just the right thing to do, so he did it. It's like asking Babe Ruth how to hit a baseball and him telling you, 'I don't know, I just hit the ball and it goes really far over the fence.' He might not be able to break it down technically, but he was the best ever at what he did, and there are a lot of guys like that in our business. When we bring in new trainers, everyone here works with them and we see who relates to whom. We see what their skill set is, we see what they have to contribute, and if I think they have what it takes to contribute—if they're the right person—then I want them to be a part of this process. If not, then I don't want them here.

"Norman Smiley is a phenomenal coach for the basics. He's just awesome. He relates to the new talent, he's easy to understand, and everybody raves about him. Do I think Norman will ever teach anything other than that? Probably not. And that's not a knock at all, because if you ask me who is one of the most valuable guys here, I'd say Norman. He is so good at teaching the basics, he doesn't need to grow out of that role—he's phenomenal. It's a basic step, but without step one, you can never get to step two. You need those basics to build on.

"Everybody has a skill set that they're great at, and you try to exploit what they're great at to bring out the best in the talent. Some guys just have a connection with the talent and will teach them the right thing in order to get them over the top."

Ask NXT talent about great coaches, however, and the one name that pops up most is William Regal. As a former WWE Superstar and a man who battled addiction problems in the past, he knows what a rough road the life of a Superstar can be, and he sees his role in the Performance Center as someone who helps shape the talent both inside and outside the ring. He wants to teach each and every talent the

Marcus Louis works on the basics with coach Norman Smiley.

Billy Gunn oversees a young Enzo Amore.

importance of what it means to be a representative of WWE.

"It's of vital importance to make sure this industry continues and to ensure the continued success of WWE," says Regal. "You have to constantly feed the system and find talent and find people who can adapt to what we do. There is only so much talent out there and not everyone is cut out for what we do. Some people can't stand the lifestyle. A lot of people think they can, but there's a big difference between performing on weekends or a couple of times a month and performing 20 times a month while traveling the world. You have to mentally prepare people. How are we changing things? The whole process is constantly evolving. We get to teach people our company's ideas as they come to NXT, so when they get to *Raw* and *SmackDown Live*, they head to the main roster with the right ideas and the right mindset. Professionalism is a big thing, and I think a lot of people don't get that. This isn't just about working for 15 minutes a day. It's about carrying yourself like a Superstar. You have to act and behave like a Superstar to work for this company, and it's not just how you act inside the ring. It's about being able to represent the company 24 hours a day. We get to start everybody the right way here, and it's crucial.

"Me and Robbie [Brookside] are the only two carnie wrestlers left in the entire industry, and we have been for years, but we never acted like that. Unfortunately, it just seemed to be the norm to act a certain way, but if you're going to be a WWE Superstar, you need to conduct yourself as a professional, inside the ring, outside the ring, on camera, off camera, and in public. So we teach these kids how to conduct themselves in a positive way and certainly not with bad attitudes. We can't have people with bad attitudes."

So while the talent is advancing from one stage to the next, the coaches are not only looking at their performance and their promos, but they're also assessing whether or not the individual has what it takes to be a modern-day WWE Superstar. It's a role head coach Matt Bloom takes very seriously. "The thing that Mr. Regal and Paul have taught me is that this business is so opinionated. There is no right way or wrong way to do things—but there *is* a WWE way," says Bloom. "We are able to provide the proper foundation to mold these talents, so that one day, hopefully, they can walk down a *Raw* ramp or a *Smack-Down Live* ramp—because that's the end game here. Everyone who comes through these NXT doors, whether they tell you or not, wants to walk down that ramp. So when we help them build a foundation based on what we expect, that helps out so much. Back in the day, you had to come from a wrestling school to make it in this business, and we still get a lot of people who come to the Performance Center from a wrestling school, but we have to remodel the habits they've learned. I'm not saying what they were originally taught was wrong, but what they were taught is not the WWE way. The beauty of what

Former WWE Superstar Steve Keirn working with Big Cass and Solomon Crowe.

we're doing now is that we recruit from all over the world, from amateur wrestlers to Olympians to pro football players to strong men—the list goes on and on. We're able to model that foundation all right here. They come to the Performance Center and we get eyes on them 24/7, we see what they're doing, how their growth is going, and what needs to be improved.

"I take a lot of pride in the training. Managing their skill level is one thing and managing their personalities is another thing. I'm trying to keep classes conducive to learning and keeping them hungry."

To do this, Bloom breaks up the classes among skill levels while leaving some advanced students in the more remedial classes. This helps the younger talent work their skills up to the next level.

Billy Gunn has some encouraging words for his eager students.

"We can't have people with bad attitudes."

"I typically break it up," he says. "There's a beginners' class, there's the women's class, then we have intermediate 1, intermediate 2, and advanced. Then we have our polishing class, which is for the talent who are getting ready to be called up to the main roster. But there are some talent in intermediate 1 who could be advanced; they understand their role is to bring up other people. If they're the best in that class, they're never really going get any better until they bring up other people. A talent can understand what we're coaching them, but to me, they truly grasp it when they can teach it to someone else—that's when they really start understanding it on a deeper level—so they're there to teach the younger kids. So even though there is a beginner, intermediate 1, intermediate 2, advanced, and polishing, there are a couple of talents in each class who are probably above that level, but it's all designed to make everyone better."

And to Bloom, it's not just about the coaching inside the Performance Center, it's about the competition the environment breeds. "Competition brings out the best in anyone," he says. "Throughout my career in athletics, I've always thrived off competition. If there's no competition, there's no will to get better, so, you know, we all help each other out. We all want the best for each other, but it's competitive to get on our live events, to get called up to the main roster, to have the best match of the night. There is competition in the weight room to have the best squat or the best bench—that brings out the best in people and I love that. I want that from our guys—friendly competition– and we have that; it's awesome because we want our talent to do well, and other talent want them to do well. But by the same token, we're gonna give you a clap on the back because now it's my turn to go out and I'm going to one-up you."

One-up the competition enough times, and the talent will begin to work with Taylor, who is known in the Performance Center as the finishing coach. "Every talent has to go to each coach. Think of each coach as a territory. Each of them has their own specialty," explains

Female trainees hone their skills with coach Sara Amato.

Taylor. "Some are highfliers. Some are athletes. Some use an intricacy of techniques. Adam Pearce is a thinking man—he knows how to create situations that become compelling storylines. Matt Bloom is 6-foot-8, 350 pounds, and a bruiser; he can teach you how to be a big man. Sara Amato teaches the girls how to do what the female talent do. We have a coach for everybody. Robbie Brookside signed from England; he knows every hold, every submission. So each talent goes through each stage and goes to each coach to learn the different aspects of our profession. They can pick up whatever fits with their character, their presentation, and they can keep what doesn't in their repertoire in case they ever need it later.

"When they get to me, I take all that and then teach them how to do television, how to work the hard camera (the camera that shows the television audience most of the in-ring action), who their character is, what moves fit their character, what presentation shows that character in the best light. When they're done with me, we can present to Vince McMahon a talent who has a move set, who has a character, who has a catch phrase—they have everything they need to go on television and not spend six months trying to figure out who they are. They go up there, and sometimes it hits, sometimes it doesn't. The New Day started out as good guys who nobody liked, and then they were bad guys who people booed so much, they started to like them again. You just never know. Present something to the audience and they'll decide, but our job is to get people as ready for television—as ready for the big time and the WWE roster—as they can be."

To Kevin Owens, the coaches' diversity is what really makes the Performance Center and NXT tick. "Robbie Brookside worked for years in England," says Owens. "Norman Smiley worked for years in Mexico, Matt Bloom worked for years in Japan, Billy Gunn was in WWE for years, and Terry Taylor came up in the territory days. Sara Amato is probably the best at what she does in the world, and she is training these girls the right way. So every coach has something different from their path that they can bring to people. And I thought that

Coach Sara Amato demonstrates a hold with future Women's Champion Paige.

was the coolest part; everyone has a different vision, a different way of doing things, but nobody is wrong, nobody is right—they all just bring to you what they can bring to you. And then you pick and choose, use what you can, use what applies to you, use what you think will be useful. To have all these resources in one place is amazing."

Bayley believes the coaches at the Performance Center have brought her abilities to a level she didn't even know was possible, helping her shake "bad wrestling habits" she learned pre-FCW/NXT. "The people that I learned from were amazing and I owe them everything; they taught me the fundamentals and drilled them into my head, which is what I believe got me here and got me a lot of opportunities elsewhere. But there are certain things that I learned here that I didn't think about, like working to a camera," she says. "Of course I didn't think about that or ring positioning or where you do certain things or how you position yourself so that the camera can see you . . . and I remember one of my first critiques was from Sara Amato, and she told me to stop forearming so much. At the time, we had to be Divas, and you didn't want to punch someone in the face because it's not the girly thing to do; that's changed now, but when I first got here I had to break that habit and learn a lot of TV stuff that I had no idea about, and they just taught me and worked me through it. It made me look like a star."

But it's not just inside the ring where Bayley had to learn the ropes. "I think I've grown from a little kid tomboy to a decent Superstar," she says. "Honestly, I didn't know how to do my makeup; I didn't know how to curl my hair; I didn't know how to straighten my hair; I never wore dresses unless I really needed to. But I had to be in a dress on my first day here, and I didn't know what was too much and I didn't know what wasn't enough. And I felt like I had to be this super Diva, so I went out and bought this little dress and somebody approached me and was like, 'You cannot wear that.' I said, 'Okay,' and then I wore a really long dress and the locker room was like, 'You look like a grandma.' It was just really hard for me to find the happy medium. I had to have girls curl my hair; I had to have girls put on eyelashes for me. It was really tough for me, and I think I got really emotional about it; this was not why I was here. I actually had a talk with AJ Lee during my first month. She said she had been in the same boat when she first got here, and she told me, 'You just need to do what they want you to do. You need to look the part, obviously, but you also need to be yourself and stay true to who you are—kind of meet them half way.' That really sunk in and I was like, 'Okay, I can be myself, but I also need to do my job.' So I got help from the girls, but I still stuck to what I believed in. If I thought, 'I wouldn't do that,' then I wouldn't do it. I wouldn't change who I was. So I totally grew as a person and as a woman and as a performer. I feel like it's night and day. I'll go back and watch my old matches, and I'm like, 'Oh, why did I do that?' It makes no sense—the way I moved, even the way I wore my gear—I hate it. I learned so much here, more than I ever thought I would, and it's changed the way I think and how I understand the psychology of a match. I don't know if I'm the best at it, but I feel like I've got a good grip on it, especially compared to what I used to know. Man, this has changed my whole life. Even if I left WWE tomorrow, I would be a whole new person, in the best way."

CHAPTER 6
Diamonds in the Rough

With the Performance Center open and the NXT coaching staff in place, the next step in Levesque's master plan was to fill each of the seven rings with talent from across the world, in order to complement a roster that already featured such indie talent as Sami Zayn, Adrian Neville, Kalisto, Finn Bálor, Hideo Itami, and Kevin Owens. But Levesque knew that for the long-term plan to take effect, he needed more athletes, more styles, and more unique looks, so he tabbed William Regal to perform a global search for young talent.

"We scout them, we hear about them, or we just know who they are," says Regal. "People are out there making a name for themselves, and we know who they are—not just me, but everybody knows. You end up watching them on TV or in person, then you sit down and talk to them, and if you think they have what it takes, you get them a tryout here. Same with the athletes. If you're an amazing athlete, we'll see if you have the proper look and the proper attitude. If you make it, you'll go through the same tryout system as everybody else. After a three-day tryout—if you have the personality and the ability to push through—we'll determine if you have what it takes to make it here. You learn a lot by watching people when they don't think you're watching—how they conduct themselves, if they're rude to people . . . you learn a lot. Just sit back and watch, and you'll see people act rude to people who they think might not matter; but you can't do that and expect to be a WWE Superstar. So they go through drills, and you watch their every move. Then they do promos on the last day of tryouts, and that's when

An early Performance Center staff photo including (left to right): Nick Dinsmore, Joey Mercury, Brian Duncan, Terry Taylor, Bill DeMott, Canyon Ceman, Sara Amato, Norman Smiley, Robbie Brookside, Matt Wichlinski, and Bryon Saxton.

you see if they have what it takes."

"On the physical side, it's another world," adds coach Robbie Brookside. "Regal and I have been around for over 20 years now. I stayed in England and Europe and that side of the world, and you always have an idea of what it takes to be a WWE Superstar, but until you actually jump into the water and have a go for yourself, you have no idea how physically tough it truly is. It's really tough. When I first came out here, I went to the previous facility in Tampa, and there was a fella named Freddie Flintoff. He was a hugely successful all-around cricket player; he's a national hero in England. After he retired, he was on all of these daredevil programs where he would challenge someone to Thai boxing or to jump off the cliffs in Acapulco. But he turned up at NXT and after just two days of the week-long tryout, he said he couldn't continue. He was totally surprised, but he was honest with us and said, 'I thought this was going to be easy, but I take my hat off to

Head Coach Matt Bloom addresses talent and staff.

everyone in this profession.'

"We come from an era when there wasn't a front door, or even a back door, to enter the industry . . . you had to create your own door to get this job."

"It's hard for people to imagine that when Robbie and I started, there was no such thing as a wrestling school," says Regal. "You couldn't even get this job unless you were an amateur wrestler or someone in your family was a wrestler. In our case, we went through the last remaining carnival wrestling booth in the world and got ourselves beat up because we asked to be wrestlers, but that was our way in. So you have to find out if these people can handle the physicality. And even when athletes do make it through the door, it's only the ones who develop an intense love for what we do who will stay and go on to succeed."

"We have everyone from an ex-Marine to a Canadian Common-

William Regal and Robbie Brookside share a laugh.

wealth wrestling champion. We have all this natural, raw talent that we have to mold," adds Brookside. "When William and I were coming up, we had to fight every day for what we had. We didn't have anything. Even our friends would make sarcastic comments about what we did, but we just wanted to get in the ring and wrestle because we loved it. From there, we got better, but our mission was to come to America, which William fulfilled and surpassed. When you have a love and a desire and a passion and you can pass that on and instill that love here with the talent of NXT, you're doing your job. We have to nurture them on a daily basis. They're these big strong beefcake fellas who can snap you in two in a second, but you have to teach them that learning why they're doing certain moves is just as important as learning the moves. You tell them why they have to do them and when they have to do them. You want to teach them the basics, a solid foundation in foot-work, and how to take things crisply. You also want to make sure they

Finn Bálor performs his signature entrance pose.

show emotion so people can relate to them. I was supposed to come here for only six months, but this is without a shadow of a doubt the best job I've ever had. I want to help this system, this facility, get better. William Regal's knowledge of this industry is second to none, and he passes that down."

To find the right athletes, Regal, Brookside, and the other NXT coaches put recruits through the most rigorous tryout in the business, with the Performance Center hosting tryouts three to four times per year.

"There's an old saying in wrestling: conditioning is your best hold," says Regal. "If you are not in your absolute best shape, you cannot do this. That is a constant: working out and conditioning. You can be as fit as a fiddle, but it's not the same as the up and down movements that we do. When you fall down, you need to remember to breathe because if you're holding your breath when you fall, you're going to get winded. At tryouts, we see athletes who are superior in other sports and they die a quick death in that ring. They're used to only doing their particular sport or exercising in their particular way, and then they come here with the up and down, side-to-side movements, and they fail. And you can see this failure crushes their spirit. These are athletes who aren't used to failing. Believe me, not everybody leaves here thinking this was the greatest experience of his or her life. Plenty leave shaking their heads, saying that they had no idea what this training was really all about. They had no concept of how hard the talent work. Nobody would ever say to a stuntman, 'That was an easy job,' but what we're doing is a far more physical form of entertainment. They're landing on pads. It's accepted, though, that stuntmen get beat up and what we're doing is fake. We get beat up every night in front of people.

"I think a lot of people who knock WWE don't watch it. If you watch it for half a minute, you'll see how physical it is. Athletes who come from other sports think it's going to be so easy, but then you talk to them and you break it down. Do you realize you're going to be away from home 300 days a year? This isn't a job; it's a lifestyle. If you don't like flying, this isn't the job for you. If you don't like driving 400 miles per day, you're probably not going to enjoy this. If you don't like getting four hours of sleep a night, this might not be the right occupation. But this is what we do. So in three days of tryouts, people learn an incredible amount of information, but they also learn an incredible amount about themselves as well, and that's where we start. Even the wrestlers who have worked elsewhere go through the same tryout, and even some of them are overwhelmed by what we do.

"People always ask why we don't sign up this guy or that guy— believe me, we know about everybody, but maybe this guy doesn't want to act professionally, or maybe he doesn't want to behave a certain way, or maybe they want that myth to be out there that we didn't want them. They'd rather tell the world, 'Oh, they didn't want me,' when there's a good chance we came looking. But maybe it's them who doesn't have what it takes. Everybody goes through the same system. *Everybody.* That's what it takes. You need to be resilient enough to go through this on a daily basis."

Apollo Crews remembers his tryout at the Performance Center as the most grueling, taxing experience he's ever been through in his athletic life. "It was very, very physical," he says. "I arrived Sunday night. On Monday morning, we signed all the paperwork, they took our blood pressure and did all of those types of tests, then we hit the ring. We rolled around a little bit and then we did conditioning drills in the ring, basically for three days straight. We also hit the gym with strength and conditioning coach Matt Wichlinski, and he put us through a grueling workout where we did everything from flipping tires to clean-pressing a log to burpees to pushing a sled. It was rough. You'd figure lifting weights would be easy because we're all weightlifters, but the stuff he had us doing is stuff your body isn't used to, movements that you don't do very often. I remember going back to the hotel room drenched in sweat, and I had to lie down on my bed for an hour before I could even take a shower. It was rough. It was probably one of the toughest physical things I've ever had to do.

"Our tryout was a smaller one. We started out with eight, and we

> ## "It was probably one of the toughest physical things I've ever had to do."

ended with six. Two people dropped out. I remember on the first day, people were running to the trash cans to throw up. Every day you're running through three shirts and you're drinking gallons of water just to keep your body hydrated. You're in there sweating, running through shirts, drinking your water. I had been wrestling before I did the tryout, but you could see the guys who hadn't were second-guessing themselves."

The FCW tryout system Baron Corbin went through was a far cry from Crews's experience. "It was the opposite of what they do now," he says, as he reminisces about his trip to Tampa. "I was the only guy there for the week, and they really gave me baby steps. I was working with Bray Wyatt a little bit, just trying to learn the basic things like bouncing off the ropes, rolling, and falling properly. My introduction was very basic. I didn't even get in the ring until the third day. It was more to watch and learn and see what it was all about. I also sat in on a promo class with Dusty Rhodes, and that was terrifying. I had never done anything like that before and it's totally different. That week, Bret Hart was in as a guest, so you have two iconic, legendary Superstars in front of you, along with a bunch of people you don't know. That was the toughest part: doing a promo. Every Thursday, FCW had a show

Baron Corbin displays his power and aggression during an NXT show.

at their old facility, and I went and watched that, then on Friday, they videotaped me running around the ring a little bit. So it was a walk in the park compared to what they do now. I was pretty fortunate that I didn't have to go through the rigorous tryouts that are part of NXT now. They have these extreme blowout drills where they really try to gut check the guys. I've helped the coaches with tryouts, and I can tell you, my tryout was definitely different."

To Levesque, the tryout is about more than just physical capability; each coach is looking for specific star-making attributes. "When looking for talent, the hardest thing to find, and the thing you just can't teach people, is charisma, that X-Factor," he says. "That is something that's unteachable. You can teach somebody how to be an actor and say lines. You can teach somebody how to do the moves. But can they resonate with the WWE Universe, do they have charisma, are they somebody people will pay to see? Those are the hardest things to find. So first and foremost, I look for charisma and somebody who has the 'it' factor. When people come in for a tryout, I know if they're a soccer player from England or a former NFL player or an MMA fighter, but that's all I know. Usually, I don't know anything else about them. But I can sit in my office and watch them for 20 minutes, and half the time I can tell you who is going to get in. The coaches will come back to me as a collective group and say, 'We want him and him, her and her,' and it's usually the same people who stand out due to their charisma. Every now and then, there is someone they'll argue for and say, 'Look, this kid might not look like anything special, but he's an unbelievable athlete and when you get him outside of his shell, he's got a great personality,' and we'll give that guy a chance. At the same time, there are instances when a guy will come in and will be just an unbelievable talent, but we already have three guys who do the exact same thing. Especially guys from the indies; we might get three guys who come in and have the same style, do the same moves, have the same personality, but we don't really need a bunch of the same guy. It's hard. It's a constant mix of what do we have, what do we need, and what are we looking for, while at the same time keeping our profile global and diverse. We try to find something that works on every level. Everyone loves someone different, so you try to find talent who will appeal to everyone."

Head coach Matt Bloom also thinks charisma is key, but he knows a student isn't getting in the WWE door without footwork and body control. "Can they control their body while controlling somebody else's body?" asks Bloom. "Is there any athleticism there? That's so important, because you can have all the charisma in the world, all the muscles in the world, all the desire in the world, but if you can't keep from hurting yourself, or, more importantly, keep from hurting the other guy in the ring, then we have no use for you. I'm a big footwork

Head coach Matt Bloom gives a pep talk.

guy; that's what I look for. Another thing, something that even trumps footwork, is attitude. If you're an asshole, you can't represent WWE or NXT. We have no use for you if you have a bad attitude."

But to Canyon Ceman, NXT's Vice President of Talent Development (and former professional volleyball player), the key is passion. "I believe that a world-class athlete who has charisma and passion will succeed," says Ceman. "So I consider it my job to find them. That might sound easy, but getting the message into the right hands is harder than it sounds—it's not like we're going to put an ad for it in the paper: 'Talent Wanted!' It takes a creative mindset to go, 'Okay, how am I going to get the message to those people who we think might be good for this business.' So you go to the strongman competitions, you go to football, you go to rugby, you go to the Olympics; those are the logical places. Then you also need to start thinking on another level. Where are those people in India? They might be doing Kushti or Kabaddi. Where are those people in Brazil? They might be doing Capoeira or MMA. Every country has its own set of challenges.

"So I think a personal attribute that has allowed me to succeed here is my creative adventurousness. I'm willing to think outside the box and go find that person, male or female, and get the message to them, like, 'We think you can do this and here's why, come give it a shot.' Once we find them, the next step is the tryout system and rookie orientation. In the past, when an athlete came to try out, it was just one guy sitting there who made the decision about whether or not to hire them. But we changed that at the Performance Center, adding another layer of professionalism to this machine, allowing it to function better. Now, everybody who's hired comes in through a tryout, which means every set of eyeballs in this building has seen them and they are empowered to speak about it and we decide as a group. Myself, Paul, William Regal, and Matt Bloom—that's the decision-making body. Everyone has a chance to express their opinions about the athletes coming into the system. I think that's important because the people in this industry love it and hold it very dear, and if they feel empowered to help decide who

gets to follow in their footsteps, it incentivizes them to then help the people that they brought in the door, as opposed to telling someone, 'You are making that guy a star, go!' and they're like, 'Well, I don't think he's got it.'"

Ceman's worldwide hunt for talent took him to the Middle East, enabling him to discover some raw athletes hungry to step into the ring.

"We had a very successful tryout in Dubai. We wanted to pick a location where both Middle Eastern and Indian talent could meet," says Ceman. That tryout did not yield any Middle Eastern talent, but it yielded two Indians who are now in our system. It also yielded a Dutch-Albanian Muslim MMA fighter, and that's a combo that you just don't find on trees. And that person would not have come to our tryout had we not held it in Dubai and had I not reached out to the Dubai MMA world. To me, it's a perfect example of how the candidates who are home runs don't necessarily come from where you think they are going to come from; they come from the worldwide network you've built. When it's a year and a half after I've met someone, and I get an email that says, 'Hey, I might have someone for you,' that's when I know the process is working. We've got a few guys here right now who are perfect examples of that—people who I didn't meet face to face, but I met a person who I told our vision to, and a year and a half later that person met someone who they thought could be a good fit.

"Dylan Miley is a great example of that. You will hear a lot about this guy in the future, and it could be in a main event. He is a game changer; he's a 6-foot-2, 300-pounder who looks like he was born to be a heel. I met him through a person who, frankly, wasted our time at a tryout. Seriously, this guy was like dead space, but we treated him with respect and we told him the truth, like, 'Look, this is not going to happen for you and here's why.' He wrote me back and said, 'You know what? Thank you, someone needed to tell me that.' But a year later, I got an email from him that said, 'I got a guy for you.' And it's clear, when Dylan walks into a room, you know he's got a future here."

But not everyone has that ideal WWE big-man, big-muscled look, so Ceman has also learned to factor in more intangibles when considering development talent, citing Kevin Owens and Sami Zayn as two performers who might not possess the physical attributes of a Roman Reigns or a John Cena, but who more than make up for it with their amazing technical skills and off-the-charts personalities.

"Kevin Owens is a great example of that, right? Sami Zayn is also a great example of someone who didn't fit into the box that we may have had here before, but I consider those guys two of the people I'm proud of having brought in here because, in a way, they're a big part of how this brand has evolved," says Ceman. "The NXT brand is Sami Zayn being hired even though he's a red-headed, multi-lingual, multi-cultural Syrian-Canadian who doesn't necessarily look like a Superstar and was an indie wrestler in its truest sense. William Regal and I saw him and were like, 'He's got something.' What is it? It's his ability to tell a story in the ring that is just world-class; that overcompensates for all the other things that make you go, 'Hmm, I'm not sure.' But when you see him work, wow, he can tell a story. He always has the audience in the palm of his hand. Kevin Owens has the same ability. He always has the audience in his hand because he's just so good and so authentic. You believe everything that comes out of his mouth.

"There's a set of attributes we're looking for: size, athleticism, charisma, professionalism, work ethic, diversity. Is someone going to have all six of those? Rarely. But the smaller you are, the better the athlete you have to be, the more charisma you have to have, the better your work ethic or professionalism has to be. Sure, work ethic and professionalism can trump the other stuff when it's lacking, but you probably should have at least four of those six. And if you only have two or three, then those two or three better be amazing, and usually the amazingness is charisma or athleticism."

The rivalry between Kevin Owens and Sami Zayn intensified during their time in NXT and continues to do so on *Raw*.

CHAPTER 7
Road Warriors

After *NXT Arrival*, WWE's development system was not only on the map, it was trending worldwide. The Performance Center was up and running, the coaching staff was in place, and new recruits were being brought in from around the world for tryouts. But Paul Levesque wanted more. Vince McMahon had asked for quarterly specials, but Levesque wondered how his team would perform outside of Orlando. The fans inside Full Sail were as loud as could be, but how would the WWE Universe react if the NXT crew popped up in other cities?

In December 2014, NXT held the special event *Takeover: R Evolution* at Full Sail to critical acclaim. The show was monumental, not only for the NXT Championship win by Sami Zayn, but also because the whole program was so well received, Levesque received an offer for NXT to hold a live event at the Arnold Classic in Columbus, Ohio.

"*R Evolution* was named because it was the evolution of NXT," says Levesque. "It was a revolution, but it was also our evolution into something more. It was received so well and the fan base was so positive about it, we came out of that with a play at the Arnold Classic.

"After *R Evolution*, we went from this best-kept secret to a show everybody was talking about. I felt like that was the show that pushed us from being developmental to being a brand. That night, we were either going to remain a developmental operation or we were going to make a statement that we'd evolved into something else. That is the night when we moved on from being just a development territory."

Takeover: R Evolution was headlined by Zayn's championship win

Hideo Itami teams with Finn Bálor to battle The Ascension at *NXT Takeover: R Evolution*.

over Neville, a thrilling match between Charlotte and Sasha Banks, the debut of Kevin Owens, and a tag-team match that saw the team of Finn Bálor and Hideo Itami take on The Ascension (Konnor and Viktor). "Right after R Evolution, we went on to the Arnold Classic. We put a show on sale right before the Arnold Classic in Columbus, and we sold out the 1,500-seat venue in minutes," says Levesque. "And this was based on social media alone. We didn't even promote it. The next night, we put on a show in Cleveland, and we sold that out as well. That's when we started to realize, 'Wow, we're really selling some tickets here.'"

With WrestleMania 31 fast approaching, Vince McMahon asked Levesque to think about running a one-off NXT event the night before 'Mania in San Jose, which was about eight miles away from Levi's Stadium in Santa Clara.

"Why don't you look at doing a show that weekend," said McMahon to Levesque. "We have all those fans in that weekend, and NXT will be a big part of Fan Axxess, but why don't we see how it will do with a show of its own."

Levesque quickly arranged a show at the San Jose State Events Center, an arena he had performed at when he was on the main roster, but in the back of his mind, he was nervous about filling the 5,000-seat arena. However, his nervousness quickly disappeared as soon as tickets went on sale and again sold out almost immediately.

"The show became one of the most buzzed-about things all weekend," says Levesque. "It was the event you had to be at. Main roster stars were there: Rollins was there, Cesaro was there. Kevin Nash, Scott Hall, and Shawn Michaels came, and Stephanie and Vince came. And it was insane; the energy in that place was insane. People from Live Nation came, people from promotions in Japan came, and it just took on this whole life of its own. We came out of that San Jose event as a massive success, and that just laid the foundation for what was to come."

"NXT is a brand, and there was no better proof in the pudding than when we walked into the arena in San Jose in front of 5,200 people," says Enzo Amore. "Fans were going crazy, chanting every single word in my promo with me. Fifty-two hundred people yelling, 'S-A-W-F-T!' We held out the microphone and they spelled it out for us. Then you got out of the ring and walked back through the curtain, and you saw Shawn Michaels, Scott Hall, X-Pac, Triple H, Stephanie McMahon—even Vince McMahon was in the house that night—just sitting there, and they're talking to everybody about what we did in the ring that night, how special it was, and the growth . . . it doesn't even seem real. It's one thing to be recognized in the grocery store, it's one thing to hear your friends and family telling you how proud they are of you, but it's a whole other animal when you walk into an arena like that.

The Vaudevillans at *NXT Takeover: Brooklyn*.

You gotta take a step back and say, 'We're a part of something special here at NXT.'"

Just a few months later, Levesque decided to push the boundaries even further. He first inserted the Finn Bálor versus Kevin Owens NXT Championship match into a WWE live event from Japan entitled *The Beast from the East*, a move that established his stars alongside main-roster icons Brock Lesnar and John Cena, and then booked the next NXT live broadcast in August 2015, the same weekend as *SummerSlam*.

What he didn't realize at the time was that NXT was about to appear in the same arena as *SummerSlam* itself.

"We were supposed to be at the Izod Center, then Izod shut down," says Levesque. "Vince said, 'I really want you to put an NXT show somewhere to make it a more attractive week to the WWE Universe.' We were putting *SummerSlam* in the Barclays Center on Sunday, *Monday Night Raw* in there on Monday, and we were going to run a smaller venue down the road on Friday or Saturday. I don't remember who first said it, but somebody said, 'Why don't you guys just run Barclays?' I kind of scoffed at first because I was like, 'You're out of your mind. Absolutely not. That's a huge venue!' They came back and said, 'You know, it's not beyond reasonable. It's a scalable building. We can scale it down to about 6,000 seats,' and I thought, 'Well, we sold over 5,000 for San Jose. Maybe it is reasonable.' I have to admit, though, I had mixed emotions about it because I wanted to keep the underground feel of what we did. I didn't want to become too big too fast and bite off more than we could chew. Part of the success of NXT is that it's counter, it's different, it's underground. It feels down and dirty, just as it should.

"I didn't want to lose that, but as the prospect became more and more real, I thought, 'Well, we could do Barclays and we could scale it down and see.' We started the presale, which was very, very limited, and after one day of the presale we had sold just about everything we had put out there. I sent a note to Michelle Wilson, our Chief Marketing Officer, to give her the ticket sales for that day, and she said, 'Wow, do you think we'll be able to hit the 5,000 mark?' And I remember thinking,

'If I don't hit 5,000, then there's a serious problem because we haven't even put tickets on sale yet. And I was starting to wonder whether or not I could sell out Barclays. But at the same time, I was trying to keep everybody's expectations under control because I didn't want to sell 10,000 tickets and have everybody disappointed and say, 'Oh man, I really thought it'd sell out.' Everybody was talking about a sellout, but I was trying to manage expectations. I just kept saying, 'Look I'll be thrilled if we sold 6,000. Thrilled! If it's 10,000, I'll do backflips.'"

When tickets went on sale to the public, sales went through the roof. Six thousand, then 10,000, until finally, all 13,000-plus tickets in the Barclays Center were sold for NXT's Saturday night super show.

"It's amazing. I'm still flabbergasted by it," says Levesque. "It's on some markets internationally, but it is primarily driven by the WWE Network, which is an amazing platform, but when you consider the reach of the WWE Network versus the reach of the USA Network or another channel on broadcast television, it's small. It's the WWE Network, Hulu, and social media, and really that's it. So far, most of our ticket sales have come from social media—it's one of the things that's really cool. We've not spent much promoting these shows because it's just word of mouth and social media. That's why I put out the hashtag #weareNXT because it's as much the WWE Universe driving NXT's success as it is us. We're putting this out there, but they're telling us what to put out and they're loving it. So I feel that we are all NXT. But it still blows my mind. It is kind of surreal that in two years, we took this little 'developmental' thing that had 10 people going to show in a warehouse in Florida to a sold out show in New York City. *If you can make it there, you can make it anywhere.* I don't know if you've ever heard that, but in New York City, 13,000 seats is amazing. And on top of that, I don't know of too many acts in the entertainment world that can go into any building anywhere in the world and sell out three days back to back to back. But Saturday night NXT, Sunday *SummerSlam*, and Monday *Raw* were all in the same building and all sold out—that speaks volumes for WWE.

"It's awesome," continues Levesque, "and it's not just the one

Apollo Crews battles Tye Dillinger at *NXT Takeover: Brooklyn*.

"This era has something magical to it, and it's only going to get better."

At *NXT Takeover: Brooklyn*, Jushin "Thunder" Liger appears on a WWE ramp for the first time.

moment. It's another step in our growth. We tried the Arnold, we did San Jose, we did Brooklyn, and we did well in all of them. It continues to grow, and we're clearly established now as our own brand."

"If you would've said to me that after two years we'd be able to go to Brooklyn and perform in front of over 10,000 screaming fans, I would've told you that you were crazy," says Terry Taylor. "We have over 30 people from the Performance Center on *Raw* and *SmackDown Live*, so that proves that what we're doing is already working—I think faster than anyone expected. We're churning out talent, and that's making WWE better and making the business better. And these kids are able to live their dream; it's phenomenal to be a part of this company right now. I've been in territories that were about to go out of business and I was also in the middle of the Monday Night War, and NXT has this special feeling, almost like when the nWo and DX were on top. This era has something magical to it, and it's only going to get better. Think about

Kevin Owens is ready for his Ladder Match versus Finn Bálor at *NXT Takeover: Brooklyn*.

it, we're supposed to be developmental, but Triple H has created a competitive brand that has screaming fans clamoring to watch and spend their money on merchandise and tickets. If you're a fan of NXT, you're going to become a fan of WWE when these guys get called up. You're going to follow that talent. WWE and NXT build on each other. There's this wonderful synergy, and it gives the WWE Universe more options to watch the kind of show they like. I think that's a fantastic opportunity."

And when that Saturday night was all said and done, *NXT Take-Over: Brooklyn* had brought down the house. The event featured the debut of Apollo Crews and the only WWE match in Jushin "Thunder" Liger's legendary career. However, the event is mostly remembered for two matches so spectacular they stole not only the NXT show, but also the entire weekend. Even during Sunday's *SummerSlam*, fans throughout the arena were still talking about Kevin Owens, Finn Bálor, Sasha Banks, and Bayley.

Finn Bálor unleashes the Demon King.

"Finn and I hadn't known each other for very long. We first met in May 2014, right before we both got here," remembers Owens. "We were on the same show in England, and we both knew we were coming here. I think for the first few months we were here, we kind of leaned on each other because we both didn't know what to expect, and we got pretty close. From the moment I first saw him in England to now, one thing I admired was the connection he has with the crowd and his uniqueness. The whole painting thing started in Japan quite a while ago, but even beyond the paint, during his last few months on the independent scene before he got to NXT, he would take on different characters and create these special moments. And I think that dual personality of Finn and the demon all comes together—he gives the WWE Universe something they have never seen before."

And the match didn't disappoint, from the Demon's entrance to the high-stakes finish that saw Bálor winning in brutal fashion, thanks to a couple of super kicks to the jaw and a Coup de Grâce double-foot stomp from the top of the ladder.

Seth Rollins adds, "The Ladder Match stood out for a variety of reasons. It was an encapsulation of NXT over the last year and what it has become. You look at these two guys, Kevin Owens and Finn Bálor, who have made names for themselves outside of the WWE realm, and now they're in our universe and they're main-eventing our show on our network in front of a sold-out crowd in the sports-entertainment capital of the world. You look at what that means for our industry, not just for WWE but for our whole industry, and what is possible moving forward—as opposed to what was possible five years ago—and you realize it's groundbreaking. It's very cool to see someone like Triple H basically open his mind, open the horizon, to what NXT can become and what WWE can become. It's very indicative of that. The main event was incredible. To see guys I've known for years, who I know have the passion, get an opportunity that they wouldn't have had five or 10 years ago—to be given that stage and applauded for their effort and not held down—is a huge leap forward for everyone."

But for Rollins, while the guys put on a spectacular show, the women might have even one-upped them. "I was able to watch Bayley versus Sasha from the front row," he says. "I hadn't watched a live match

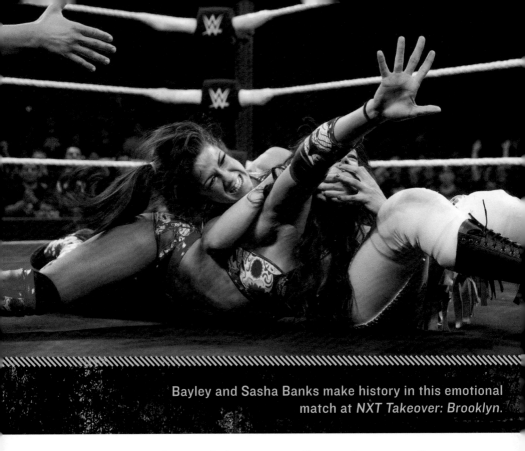

Bayley and Sasha Banks make history in this emotional match at *NXT Takeover: Brooklyn*.

as a spectator in the crowd since 2004, so for me, that was really special. Between the video package and the opening announcements of the match, I had trouble keeping it together. It was just a really special moment. And nothing against Kevin and Finn, but that women's match should've been the main event of that show. From an emotional standpoint, there was nothing even close to that the whole weekend. It was really incredible to watch the crowd be that into a women's match and how much it meant to both of them. From watching Bayley win the Championship to seeing all four of them [Bayley, Sasha, Charlotte, and Becky Lynch] in the ring afterwards, it was tough for me to hold it together emotionally, but I knew I had to be on camera shortly afterwards, so I was really just biting my lip. There were multiple times when I had to turn away because I knew if I got too invested, tears would've just flooded out of me. It was incredible to feel that way. It made me feel like a kid again."

The Essential NXT

Twenty-one matches
that helped put NXT on
the wrestling map

Big E Langston versus Seth Rollins \\ January 9, 2013

Big E captured the NXT Championship in a no-disqualification match that saw the entire NXT roster run out to combat the outside interference from Dean Ambrose and Roman Reigns.

Sami Zayn versus Antonio Cesaro // August 21, 2013

The Two-out-of-Three Falls Match that lit up social media and helped make NXT must-see TV.

William Regal versus Antonio Cesaro \\ December 25, 2013
Cesaro was not in the giving mood during NXT's Christmas special, and instead delivered punishment to the WWE legend, who was more than game for the challenge.

Sami Zayn versus Cesaro \\ February 27, 2014
The Swiss Superman took on the popular Sami Zayn to kick off NXT's first live event on the WWE Network. The epic bout was hailed by many as a Match of the Year candidate.

Paige versus Emma // February 27, 2014

This is the match that put the sports entertainment world on notice: the NXT women are here to fight. Paige won with the P.T.O.

Adrian Neville versus Bo Dallas // February 27, 2014

Neville won the NXT Championship in a brutal Ladder Match. The Red Arrow Neville performed toward the end of the bout is one of the most unforgettable moves in NXT history.

Natalya versus Charlotte \\ May 29, 2014
Two second-generation Superstars traded blows in front of legends Ric Flair and Bret Hart. Charlotte became the second-ever NXT Women's Champion with the win.

Sami Zayn versus Tyler Breeze \\ May 29, 2014
One of Breeze's biggest victories in NXT, Prince Pretty became the number one contender for the NXT Championship.

Adrian Neville versus Sami Zayn versus Tyler Breeze
versus Tyson Kidd // September 11, 2014
A furious Fatal 4-Way that saw Neville retain the NXT Championship thanks
to a swift Superkick and Red Arrow on Zayn.

Finn Bálor and Hideo Itami versus The Ascension \\ December 11, 2014
From Bálor's epic entrance (and the first appearance of the Demon) to Bálor and Itami's double-stomp finish, this hard-charging match was about as intense as they come.

Charlotte versus Sasha Banks \\ December 11, 2014
Charlotte successfully defended the NXT Women's Championship, but "The Boss" proved that she was ready to move up to the main-event scene.

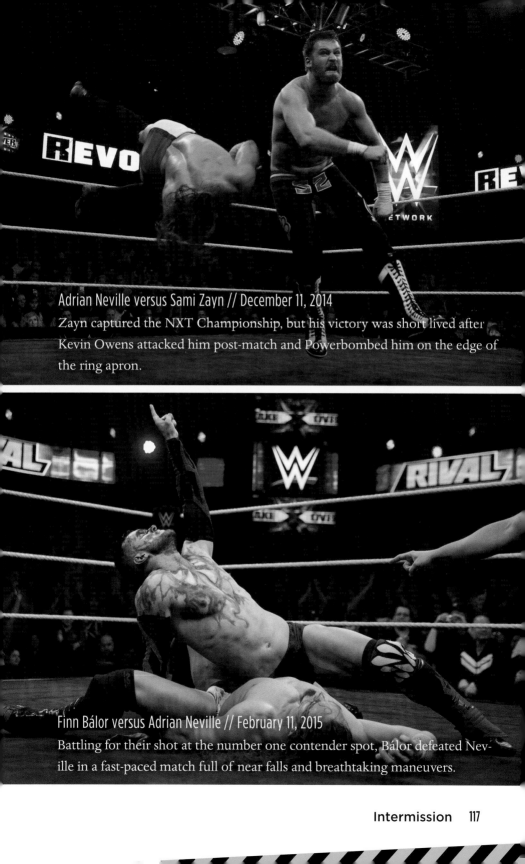

Adrian Neville versus Sami Zayn // December 11, 2014

Zayn captured the NXT Championship, but his victory was short lived after Kevin Owens attacked him post-match and Powerbombed him on the edge of the ring apron.

Finn Bálor versus Adrian Neville // February 11, 2015

Battling for their shot at the number one contender spot, Bálor defeated Neville in a fast-paced match full of near falls and breathtaking maneuvers.

Sami Zayn versus Kevin Owens \\ February 11, 2015
One of the more brutal matches in NXT history. Owens proved too powerful for Zayn after a series of Powerbombs left the champ stunned. K.O. won the NXT Championship, but the rivalry was far from over.

Charlotte versus Bayley versus Sasha Banks versus Becky Lynch \\ February 11, 2015
The Fatal 4-Way between "The Four Horsewomen" not only showed how skilled these ladies really are, but also helped propel "The Boss" to the NXT Women's Championship.

Becky Lynch versus Sasha Banks // May 20, 2015
An emotionally draining, electrifying match where character work shined just as bright as the devastating moves in the ring.

Bayley versus Sasha Banks // August 22, 2015
One of the best women's matches ever performed, Bayley and Banks put on a classic in front of thousands of screaming, adoring fans. Bayley won the NXT Women's Championship to usher in the next chapter of the NXT Women's Division.

Finn Bálor versus Kevin Owens \\ August 22, 2015

The main event of *Takeover: Brooklyn*, this was a fierce Ladder Match highlighted by competitors fighting in the stands, on the announcers' table, and, of course, off the ladder. Bálor retains the title after a crazy, hard-fought bout.

Bayley versus Sasha Banks // October 7, 2015

A 30-minute Women's Iron Man match. Bayley won three falls to two thanks to a last-second submission hold that forced Banks to tap.

Finn Bálor versus Samoa Joe // December 16, 2015

The only thing more epic than the crowd response to Bálor was the champ's ability to escape Joe's Muscle Buster and finish off the challenger with a Coup de Grâce.

Samoa Joe versus Shinsuke Nakamura \\ August 20, 2016
The King of Strong Style captured the NXT Championship after hitting two Kinshasa knee strikes, including one off the middle rope.

PART TWO
Beards, Divas, and Selfie Sticks

CHAPTER 8
We're Here

Although hundreds of students have stepped foot in the Performance Center, Paul Levesque calls Bray Wyatt, formerly known as Husky Harris, the first character fully packaged by NXT for a successful *Raw* debut. But the process that led to Wyatt's success wasn't as simple as giving him a fresh start; Wyatt dipped into everything the talent and the coaches had to offer.

"Bray began with my real-life lunacy," says Wyatt. "I've always been an against-all-authority kind of child. I was a big fan of Rage Against the Machine, they were a big influence on my life as a child, so when I started working with Dusty Rhodes, I began losing my mind on a very real level. I became obsessed with this character."

When Husky Harris failed on the main roster, he went all in with the Wyatt persona. "I was going to jury duty in my hometown, and Dusty made me go to jury duty as Bray," Wyatt says. "Dusty told me, 'This is the perfect exercise. Become Bray.' I literally went to jury duty as Bray Wyatt. I was so immersed in the character that I didn't break once. Obviously, I didn't get picked for jury duty, but I had the white pants, Hawaiian shirt, the whole nine yards. There were no fragments of Husky Harris. Husky Harris was dead, and he was to stay dead. I was Bray Wyatt. We were one.

"I remember when the coaches came to us and they were like, 'Things are changing here, guys.' We liked being out in our own little world of FCW, and we didn't like change. So we were like, 'No, no, no, this sucks.' First time we went to Full Sail, there were like 50 people

It was in NXT where Bray Wyatt's creepy persona was born.

there and we did a test run, and Hunter took over. We started gaining confidence once we saw how Full Sail was set up. It was nothing like it is now, but we had some matches, and when we came back, we were like, 'Wow, this might actually be pretty cool. We might have to move to Orlando, but this might end up being kind of cool.' A couple of months later, we started the television product, and Hunter gave us a platform where we could create and be whoever we wanted to be. I started doing the vignettes as Bray, and I took it as seriously as possible. I took it very, very seriously.

"We were all into it and we all started becoming things. We were no longer just guys who wore tights. We were becoming actual characters, and it was almost bizarre. One person saw what was working, and then everybody wanted to jump on it. At the time, the only characters were us as The Wyatt Family and The Ascension. Characters like this weren't on the main product at the time, in my opinion, and

we weren't cartoon characters. We were real. That's the best way I can explain it, and it was a real cool atmosphere the first couple of times we came out. I ended up tearing my pec, and that's when Harper, Rowan, and I became that group, and it caught fire. The crowds acted so crazy when we came out, it was almost like we were a football team and we were playing at home every single week. We felt like celebrities. For the first time, we felt like we were big stars. We were performing in this tiny room at Full Sail, but the place started coming alive. People were getting behind us, and each person who joined added something to the group. I didn't used to have the lantern, but then we came out to the music and everybody in the crowd just swayed. It was becoming this real, awesome vibe. We were no longer focused on just getting to the main roster. Now, although we wanted to get on the main roster, nobody was going to take being down here away from us."

And Wyatt realized the power of NXT the first time he brought the character to WWE's main roster. He hadn't yet appeared on *Raw*, but WWE was giving Wyatt the opportunity to work with some veterans in non-televised matches during a tour of the West Coast and Canada.

"It's funny, back then, we were still down in Orlando and detached from the world. But I was doing some live events with the main roster," he remembers. "At the time, NXT was only airing internationally in Canada and Europe. I'll never forget, I was on a loop, and my first stop was Salt Lake City, Utah. I'm busting my ass, and I come out, and no one knows who I am in Utah. I'm like, 'Okay, it's a process, it's going to take a while for people to catch on.' The next night, we go to Canada,

and I come out to the biggest pop anybody had all night. It was all because of NXT. It was the first time I realized that this thing is catching fire. This thing is real. What a difference. These people had seen me, they knew who I was, they knew what product I was pushing, and they were so excited to see me. I felt like I was back at Full Sail, in front of my home crowd. It was a really awesome feeling. It was the same thing when I debuted. My vignettes first started airing, and I guess Vince was expecting people to be like, 'Who is this mysterious character?' But that's not what happened. Across the world, Bray Wyatt was trending on Twitter, which is not something I typically care about, but I do for this instance because Vince goes, 'How the hell did they know his name?' WWE never once said my name, they never once showed my name in the vignette, but everyone knew my name because of what Hunter had done at NXT. What a feeling. It was transcending. I was welcomed because of all the hard working people at NXT. People were now appreciating and getting behind what is now an empire and a dynasty. It was just beautiful.

"A couple of weeks later, we came back to NXT, and to this day, our NXT return is my favorite moment of my career. We came out to the lantern video and I said, 'NXT, we're home.' It was home. And we come out to this crazy noise, and then I cut my epic promo to NXT. It was a thank you for everything they did for us. The Wyatt Family loves you, and The Wyatt Family will be back. It was almost like if Shawn Michaels retired in front of a tiny building; it was just that kind of moment you can't recreate, even if you wanted to. To see what NXT has grown into and what it has become is just incredible. To see these guys at the Barclays Center and going on UK tours, it's unbelievable. There's a little part of me that's like, 'Man, I feel great for these guys, but I wish I could still be a part of this.' We have a little joke where we consider ourselves to be the grandfathers of NXT. We were the first package to come up completely as is. We walked straight out of the pages of a comic book, but our comic book was NXT. NXT helped introduce us to the world. It was really cool."

Luke Harper and Erick Rowan pose with the NXT Tag Team titles.

Wyatt credits the team of coaches for helping not only his character, but also his growth as a performer.

"I definitely spent a lot of time with Dr. Tom Prichard (former head trainer at Deep South Wrestling and FCW), and he was a huge influence," says Wyatt. "He taught me how to loosen up and how to flow freely. He taught me to not be afraid to try things, which is absolutely imperative. You have to go out there and create and not be forced to stick to a structure. I can't let someone else tell me who I am; only I know who I am. It was the Wild West down in FCW—we did what we wanted and that kind of carried over in our attitude. We want it, and we want it now, and we want it all—that was our attitude. Joey Mercury spent a lot of time crafting my movements and making sure I didn't go too far. I have a way of doing that; especially back then when there were no rules. There was no telling what I was going to say, no telling what I was going to do. That's what made me.

"I was so frustrated with people trying to put a label on me and trying to make me something I wasn't. The Bray Wyatt character was something I was thinking about and something I wanted to try, and I completely changed everything before I did it the first time. I covered up my tattoos; I got new tattoos over my old ones just so I'd be different. I grew out my hair, I grew out my beard, and when I came out to do it the first time in promo class, I remember there was just complete silence. I didn't really know how it went. Then Dusty clapped his hands together, and all of my peers started clapping for me. Right then and there, Dusty said, 'This is you, isn't it?' It was me. I knew it. Dusty knew it. We all knew it. I had prepared character stuff for Bray six months before Bray ever set foot in any arena. I put everything into it. It was all or nothing. It was this risqué character, and it could've ended at any moment because it was so out there and so against the grain. Or it could've exploded and started an empire. I'm happy to say that thanks to Hunter and Dusty, all of my wildest dreams came true."

According to Wyatt, the true game changer was the first vignette he ever shot. "I don't know how much vignettes cost, but I imagine they're very expensive to shoot," says Wyatt. "But I knew we didn't need fancy cinematography to make us look cool. We already knew our image and who we were and what we wanted to talk like. We went out and shot tests. We went out to the woods where I grew up and there was no script. Dusty just said, 'Tell me how you feel, kid.' So I stood up in the middle of the woods and I started ranting and raving and it was all 100 percent genuine because it was all 100 percent real. We shot a ton of images, and I had bought Erick Rowan this lamb mask and I said, 'This is just a beautiful metaphor for everything. This lamb mask tells a story.' We had been told the lamb mask would never work. I'm not going to mention names, but we were told not to use the lamb mask. They said it would never go over on TV. But when we were out in the woods, Dusty goes, 'Hey, Rowan, did you bring the lamb mask?' And Rowan goes, 'Yeah, got it right here.' So he put on the lamb mask and the rest is history. We shot those vignettes on a handheld camera for a couple of buckets of fried chicken. There was no camera crew. There were two guys and the Wyatts. We went out into the woods and they let us be us, and that's what Vince saw. They knew that they could put all this money behind the video and put us in some crazy atmosphere, but what we shot was so genuine and it was so unlike anything else, Vince was like, 'It can't get any better than this.' What a pat on the back that was to us."

But Wyatt wasn't the only reclamation project going on inside the Performance Center. Another Superstar who successfully changed both his character and fortune in NXT is Tyler Breeze.

"I was working as Mike Dalton, and I wasn't really getting much traction down there," says Breeze. "I was spinning my wheels, and even though I was working with everybody, my character wasn't really taking off. There just wasn't much substance to it. If you asked me who Mike Dalton was, I really had no clue. I would just go out there and try to entertain some people. Maybe it worked, maybe it didn't, but basically it came to a point where they told me, 'We need something we can market. We need to sell something about you, otherwise we don't need you around.'"

Tyler Breeze snaps a quick selfie.

Breeze sat down with roommate Xavier Woods, and the two spent a weekend brainstorming characters.

"I need to do something or I'm out of here," Breeze told Woods.

Woods responded, "Well, worst-case scenario is that they follow their plan to get rid of you, so let's give it everything we've got so you have no regrets."

"The last thing you want to do is get released and then sit around and think about all the things you should've tried," says Breeze. "So basically, for a full week, I just started coming up with different characters. I actually came up with 10 different characters all with different names, different looks, and different personalities. I wrote a paragraph on each one, what they were all about, what motivates them—everything I could think. I showed them to Xavier and asked him what he thought. From there, we chose the three best, then we spent the entire weekend at our place in downtown Tampa, just filming little trailers

"I need to do something or I'm out of here."

about who each character is and what you could expect from them. I emailed them out to everyone I could think of, and as soon as I emailed them out, I heard back from Dusty, and he told me, 'Hey, there might be something to this model character. Let's talk more about it on Monday.' I went in and we had a promo class, and I started to test out a few of the characters in front of everyone, and the model got the biggest response from everybody. Dusty and Bill DeMott took an interest in it and thought it was really cool, so we started to get rid of Mike Dalton, get him off TV, and recreate what I would end up being. It took a while to put the finishing touches on it, but that was the jump-off point. It was actually very different to what it is now.

"It's really a collaborative effort to create a character like this. Without Dusty, it never would've gotten off the ground. Billy Gunn and Bill DeMott helped navigate where the ring work was going. We'd try something, then we'd get rid of it, then we'd try something else and see if that worked better. For example, we started with a hand mirror, and it took about six months of fine-tuning behind the scenes before we finally got the go ahead to debut, and the production team really played a big role in my entrance as we figured out how to stream my phone onto the Jumbotron. We added the selfie stick, and everything

started evolving really quickly. So the idea of who Tyler Breeze is, that was my baby, but the whole production of what you see wouldn't be possible without the help of so many people."

Some of the best advice Breeze received was from Levesque, who replaced the hand mirror Breeze was walking into the ring with, with a cell phone. Levesque told Breeze, "I think the selfie is so huge right now, and it's only going to get bigger, so let's tap into that."

"The mirror was an '80s wrestling gimmick, and his idea was to make it more modern," adds Breeze. "So we switched it, and it really took off. Then when we did Brooklyn, we were able to do the Facebook and Periscope Live stuff, and that had never been done before. I had three phones going—the WWE account, the NXT account, my account—and they were all streaming, so you could log on to any one of those accounts and see different views of the entrance. There were tens of thousands of people who logged on to see, and that showed a huge interest in not only the product, but also my character. It's something different that people hadn't tapped into yet, so it was cool that I got to introduce that. Technology is just advancing so quickly that what I'll be able to add to my character moving forward is just unlimited."

When Apollo Crews joined NXT after a successful run on the independent scene, he quickly learned that the key to character creation and being able to stand out in a roomful of WWE hopefuls is the ability to be yourself when the camera lights are on.

"I'm thankful because I don't have to deviate too far from who I actually am," says Crews. "I've heard from other people that I have the ability to go out there and just be me. Nobody can be me better than I can be myself, so in the end, that's all I know. I don't have to find or play a character who's not really me. When I was growing up, the guys I liked to watch did the same thing. They were themselves, just on a bigger scale. It's me being myself, just adding a little extra to it. The name I used in the independents was Uhaa Nation, and I knew I had to change my name, and I was a little bit worried about that, but Apollo was a name I really wanted. That was my first choice when I came

Baron Corbin becomes the Lone Wolf in NXT.

With his true self unleashed, the Lone Wolf begins to dominate.

in, so when I was able to get that, I was extremely happy. I was lucky. Sometimes you get stuck trying one thing, which may not work, and then you have to try and think of something new, and who knows if that will work or if it's too late. I was one of the lucky ones."

Baron Corbin agrees. After trying a few different gimmicks throughout the development process, he found his true character when he took a closer look inside himself. "The main guys who helped me were Dream and Billy Gunn," says Corbin. "Billy Gunn was my right-hand man. He really helped me find myself both inside and outside of the ring. Dream really helped me convey it to an audience. Those two guys played an unbelievable role in what I've become. I played with a few different things when I was trying to find myself, but it just wasn't working. My promos weren't believable, and I struggled. Dream and Billy were both like, just go up and be yourself. I'm kind of a salty person; I definitely stick to myself. My whole thing of being the Lone Wolf is really just how I am. I don't hang out with people from here, I really just have my core group of family and friends and that's it. So I started doing promos as myself, and Baron Corbin is basically just an exaggerated version of who I really am. These are my feelings and what I believe, and that's the easiest thing for me to do. The more ways I can express myself, the more my character can evolve and become so much more well-rounded and offer more opportunities. And the people believe it because it's real. I like to fight and I'm a loud mouth who likes to talk trash. If you look me up on the internet, you'll see that I was fighting for my NFL career, and I was literally getting in fist fights on the practice field in the NFL and in college.

"When you are who you are, it gives you longevity. We all change through our endeavors, through our struggles, through our successes, and our character is going to do the same thing, so if you're being yourself, it will just naturally evolve."

Being yourself has also worked for breakout stars Finn Bálor and Kevin Owens.

"When I came in, I was getting a lot of advice and a lot of direction from different people," says Bálor. "You try to listen to everybody, but at the end of the day, you have to be true to yourself and true to what you believe in. People gave me some good advice, and I'd take that and run with it . . . but other people would offer things that weren't really me, so I just set that aside. One of the guys who gave me great advice is Road Dogg. I remember the day of my debut, I saw him and asked, 'Do you have any advice?' And he told me, 'Finn, just go out and be you.' And that's been my NXT motto ever since. If it feels right to me, then that's what I'm going to do—that's really the best advice anyone has ever given me. I've gotten a lot of input from Terry Taylor and Matt Bloom, who are two of the best coaches I've ever worked under. Triple H is another person who has given me great advice. Those four men have been hugely influential in what I've done so far in my NXT career.

"When I first made the move to NXT, a lot of my friends in the UK and Japan said, 'What are you doing? They're going to give you a green beard and a leprechaun sidekick.' I had been in NXT a couple of months when I decided that the body paint could be done here, so I had a meeting and was blown away that Hunter wanted me to try it at

"Just go out and be you."

Finn Bálor's "Jack the Ripper" entrance at *NXT Takeover: London.*

NXT. Obviously, it's something that's very elaborate and extravagant, especially when you add the smoke and pyro, and it's a huge team effort to make it look as cool as it does. It's more fun for the fans, and it's more interesting to me. The fans are waiting, wondering what I'm going to come out as, so it makes it fun. There's a lot more to this industry than what goes on in the ring; there's a showmanship to it. We're painting a picture, so I said, 'Why don't I start painting on myself?' I pitched it to one of my best buddies when I was in Japan, and he told me, 'That's going to suck. It's going to be a big mistake, don't do it.' But I did it at the biggest show of the year in front of 40,000 people. I covered myself in paint from head to toe, and the crowd was really into it. It was supposed to be a one-time thing, but now it's become one of the things I'm most known for."

Owens adds, "Yeah it's all very genuine. It took me 14, 15 years to get here, and I'm glad I'm here, but in a way I'm annoyed that it took me so long. I think I should have been here six years ago. But I don't know if it took people that long to recognize what I could bring to the table or if it took me that long to be valuable and to bring something

Sasha Banks becomes "The Boss" in NXT.

that's beneficial for everybody. But everything you see when I'm in front of the cameras, or even right now, is very genuine. I remember when I got to the Performance Center, one of the first things that Dusty wanted to do was sit in a room with me, turn on a camera, and just talk. The first thing I talked about was my family and my kids and my wife, and about 15 minutes later, Dusty turned off the camera and said, 'Well, whatever we do with you, your family is going to have to come through because that is who you are.' I'm a pretty genuine person and sometimes it is good and sometimes it is bad—it's not always positive, but I am who I am. That is the one thing I have always said: I am who I am. It might not always work to my advantage, but it has done me well so far. I feel like trying to be something else wouldn't work, so here we are."

When it comes to the female talent in NXT, the women are not just trying to hone their own personalities, they're attempting to stand out from the women of *Raw* and *SmackDown Live* and distinguish themselves, both in and out of the ring.

"I thought of so many different things. I thought of this crazy girl, I thought of this nerdy chick who loved anime, but I just thought, 'How can that click with the audience?' says Sasha Banks. "I also really thought about what we were missing. And at the time, we didn't have any bad guys and we didn't have any guys who were over the top and cocky, which you really don't see with girls in general, and I just sat down and thought, 'What's around you? What's hip right now? What's big?' All the big things were Nicki Minaj, Kanye West, Floyd Mayweather, and I just put those personas together and I tried to make something of my own. And I just thought, 'You know, you're related to [Snoop Dogg], someone pretty famous, and people can relate to that. So there you go: there's your background story, there's your character.' The best thing you can do is try. You either fail or you'll always wonder . . . so I kept trying." Banks scrunches up her face and says, "I remember when I started that character, people gave me that face. But I felt comfortable with it and that was the first time that I ever really

felt comfortable doing something. I remember Dusty told me to keep doing it and to keep working on it, and every week I would come to promo class with a new promo and a new idea for the character and even crazier and blingier outfits, and it just finally clicked. And now Sasha Banks has taken off."

As for Bayley, she says her character is simply her times 50,000. "Or me as a 10-year-old or any other 10-year-old girl who loves WWE," she explains. "I get to be myself—it's awesome. I get to perform how I want to perform; I really do love bright colors, and I get to put whatever I want on my gear. I played basketball as a kid, so I always tied up my hair. My mom used to fix my hair before school and as soon as I got to school I would take it all out and put it in a ponytail. I was such a tomboy. But I was taught to keep everything inside and be professional. Especially working here, I want to be professional. But when I'm out there, I get to let it all out and I can add everything I felt as a kid into my character. So I just go back and think about certain things, like how I felt when I met certain Superstars, how I felt when I met Matt Hardy or Kurt Angle or John Cena, and then I bring that out and channel it into what I'm doing now."

And that includes her trademark colors. "I love bright colors!" she says. "Everybody just does one plain color, but I just love all kinds of colors. Maybe some people think it's weird, but I just love it, and it makes people happy. I feel like when you see something bright it makes you feel happy, which is what I want to do."

CHAPTER 9
Role Reversal

NXT talent receive tutorials on more than slams and submissions. Everyone in the Performance Center building is also given time behind the mic in order to learn how to call matches as an announcer. For up-and-coming talent Corey Graves, it was a lesson that eventually led to a full-time position within WWE after a series of concussions meant his in-ring career was in jeopardy.

"I had absolutely no idea I would become an announcer," says Graves. "When I got my last concussion, during what would turn out to be my last match ever, it was at *Axxess* in New Orleans before *WrestleMania*. I remember after *WrestleMania*, I couldn't work for a few months, and one day I was sitting down with Michael Cole, and we were just chatting, and he said, 'Hey, do me a favor. When you get back to the Performance Center, try jumping into the commentary booth.' Before then, I hadn't spent much time in there. I was part of the talent. I wanted to be a Superstar. Little did I know that the time spent in there would end up saving my career at WWE. I didn't know it at the time, but my in-ring career was over. So while I couldn't be in the ring, I needed something to do, so I spent hours on end in the commentary booth calling matches with Rich Brennan. Who knew it would pay off big time?

"There was a ton to learn, though. I've watched WWE my entire life, and I assumed that being a commentator wasn't that hard. You just talked about what was going on. But to then learn all of the little nuances—like why you talk about what you do, when to remind the

NXT commentators (left to right): Alex Riley, Mauro Ranallo, and Corey Graves.

WWE Universe about certain things, how to be subtle and tell stories and not over talk and let certain things breathe—I learned there's actually way more to doing commentary than I ever realized."

Graves had been working on his commentary skills for a few months when WWE doctors told him that the concussions he'd suffered were severe enough to end his days inside the ring. "I was at a crossroads. I had been working in the booth and doing commentary to keep myself busy; it hadn't been the career I was pursuing," remembers Graves. "It was more to keep myself occupied and learn something in case I ever needed something else to fall back on. The whole time I was hurt, I was trying to learn anything and everything about the business that I could. I would sit for hours with Dusty in his office, talking and working on promos. Then eventually, I tried to learn production, and music, and lighting . . . just anything I could, and what is amazing is all of

Corey Graves reinvents himself as a commentator in NXT.

these things can be learned at the Performance Center. There are all of these aspects of the business that I was able to expose myself to. These aren't things that were forced upon me or offered up on a platter; I had to work and search it out. There are so many different things that are a part of this business that I had no idea about, from commentary to television production, so I set out to learn everything I could. I jumped with both feet into everything. So when I was eventually shut down, Triple H came to me and said, 'We're going to give you a chance. It's not your fault what happened to you. You didn't screw up, but you don't have forever to learn something else.' So I looked at everything, and, eventually, commentary caught on.

"When I started to learn commentary, I didn't put all of my effort and concentration into it because I thought that sooner or later I would be jumping back into the ring. I didn't really study too much at first, but what amazed me was how much I retained from watching WWE over the years. I was always a huge fan of Jesse Ventura and Bobby Heenan; they're my all-time favorites. I think that I have a little bit of that flavor, and it's not intentional, but people will point it out to me, and that makes sense because those guys have been my favorites forever. Now I turn on the WWE Network and put on a pay-per-view from the late '90s or early '80s, and I won't even watch the matches, but I'll listen to the commentary as I'm doing things around the house. Cole and some of the producers have also been awesome in helping me. They'll sit there and give me advice, but a lot of my success has really just come from my ability to be myself. When I was Corey Graves the wrestler, I had to be a badass at all times. But now, it's okay to be a sarcastic goof and make fun of things and entertain myself; luckily, it seems to be translating pretty well."

Graves's transition worked so well and so fast in part because of all the tools available inside the Performance Center, including a system called VBrick. It enables Graves, or any wannabe announcer, to request just about any match they can think of, then lend their voice to the action.

"We can make a few phone calls and they can send down pretty much any match in our archives," says Graves. "We can cue it up and just voice-over all of the commentary. Rich and I would sit in there for hours watching old matches from the main roster and from NXT, and to this day there are some matches I never want to see again because we did commentary on them over and over and over. They were just NXT throwaway TV matches, but it was what we had readily available. So we'd call that same match and we'd try to call it different ways. I'd be pro one guy, then we'd watch it over, and I'd call it a different way the second time. It's just all about repetition. The VBrick system is pretty awesome, and it gives us access to so many matches. We'd cue up pay-per-view main events days after they happened and put our spin on it, do the commentary our way, and see how it would come out. We would also do all of these Performance Center shows where guys who didn't work on the live show or guys who were working on something new would come in, and they would do live matches; the audience would be only the boys. We would all sit down and crowd around the ring, and some of us would do commentary during those matches. It's all about repetition. The more matches you see, the more you practice, the better you get."

And as Graves improved, he got the call he was hoping for—Levesque offered him a full-time gig to continue his career in NXT as a commentator.

"At first, it was a sigh of relief—I have a family that depends on me. Although I'd worked my whole life to be a WWE Superstar, at least I'm still in the business and with the company I've always aspired to work with," says Graves. "In a weird way, I've been offered more opportunities now than when I was a talent. I get to do a lot of really cool things, and the company lets me do a lot of media and appearances—it's been awesome. I'm having a great time, but I'm not going to lie, I miss being in the ring every day. When we were in Brooklyn—being ringside and hearing how rabid the crowd was—it was bittersweet. But I've learned to feed off of the audience's energy while doing commentary. And to

Corey Graves at the *Hell in a Cell* kickoff show.

this day, that's the hardest thing for me. When the crowd is down, doing commentary is tough. But when the crowd is fired up, and in NXT they almost always are, then I'm a fan again.

"I get to look at the business in a different way. If I'm saying great things about someone on commentary, it's because I genuinely enjoy them. I'm very rarely forced to say nice things about someone who I don't truly believe in. I'm not forced to say things, so I get to act accordingly. It's real. When someone does something that entertains me as a fan, I can convey that. There's not this façade that I need to keep up like when I was a talent who was trying to be a tough guy. Corey Graves the Superstar wouldn't blab about this, but now I get to be myself and I get to talk about the people who truly entertain me."

CHAPTER 10
Giving Back

Austin Aries. Samoa Joe. Rhyno. Tyson Kidd. Zack Ryder. Cesaro.

When you think development system and wrestling school, those aren't the first names you'd think of as talent who need to work on their craft. But NXT isn't about pitting rookie against rookie and seeing what happens. Every match has a purpose, and to some development talent, the biggest opportunity they could get is the chance to step inside the ring and compete against someone who is more experienced and who can give them some on-the-job, between-the-ropes training.

Paul Levesque explains, "When I started, I was as green as grass—I didn't know what I was doing. WCW offered me more money to stay, but Vince was offering me an opportunity. That's why I left WCW and came here. Eric Bischoff said to me, 'We're not going to run house shows anymore. You only have to work a couple of days a month.' Vince said to me, 'If you come here, you're going to work 300 days a year and you'll get the chance to work with everybody.' That's what did it for me. I didn't care about making money. I just wanted to be great at this, and to do that, I needed to do this every night and I needed to work with everybody, especially people better than me. Vince said, 'I guarantee you, you'll get your chance to do that.'

"You have to work with people better than you if you want to get better. That's just the way it is, so that's why we've started bringing in veteran performers to work with the newer NXT talent. I had a conversation with Rhyno when he was working the indies, and he's very much about helping out the younger guys. So I said, "Great, I can bring

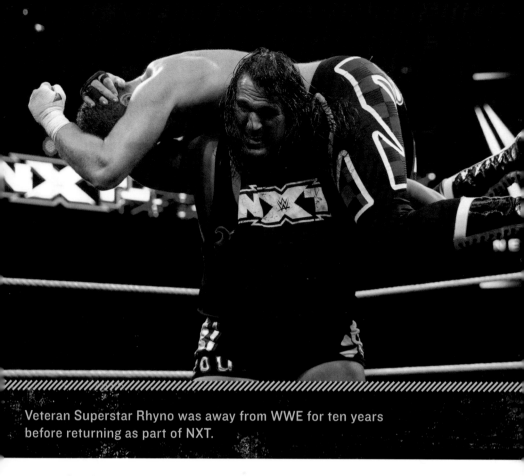

Veteran Superstar Rhyno was away from WWE for ten years before returning as part of NXT.

him here, I can rub him up against a couple of guys like Baron Corbin, and it will make the NXT guys better. You look at Corbin, he's from the NFL and doesn't have the same type of experience that a lot of guys have. He takes a lot of grief from people on the internet because he didn't come up through the indies, but he is really good and has a ton of charisma. The WWE Universe hasn't seen what he can do yet, and I'm milking their reaction by not unleashing everything he can do. I can book him with guys like Rhyno, and he can go out and prove himself for 15 or 20 minutes. Corbin went out and looked good with Rhyno, then he followed up and looked good against Samoa Joe, another veteran. Would Corbin be making these same strides against people with less experience? Probably not. At this point, he's still learning, but by putting him in the ring against guys like Joe and Rhyno, that rub helps not only in the eyes of the WWE Universe, but also in his

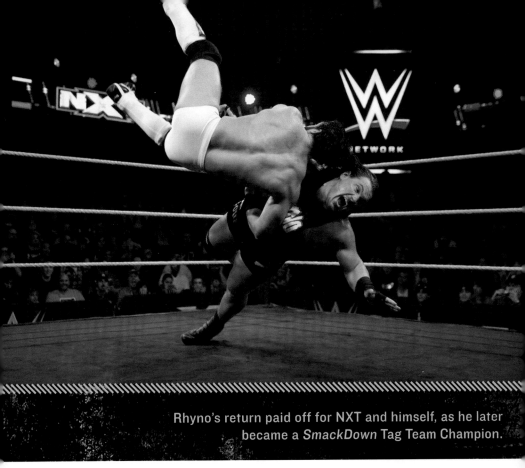

Rhyno's return paid off for NXT and himself, as he later became a *SmackDown* Tag Team Champion.

work in the ring—it helped Baron Corbin, it helped Tyler Breeze, and it helped Sami Zayn. Working with guys with more experience makes you a better performer, and as long as I'm staying honest to what NXT fans want, I'm going to continue to do it. Some of the Universe look at Rhyno coming in or Samoa Joe coming in and try to say that NXT is no longer about development, but that's exactly what it is. Did you enjoy the match? It's a product. Sometimes I book talent against veterans just to give them the chance to learn. I'm not bringing in Rhyno because I think Rhyno is going to be in *WrestleMania* next year. Rhyno is smart enough to know that being on television makes him hot, and putting him in NXT makes him hot again. Putting him on TV drives his price back up—he makes more money; he gains more popularity. It works for him; it works for me. It's a good thing."

It's also an advantageous play for veterans like Tyson Kidd, Cesaro,

and Zack Ryder, who might be getting overlooked on the main roster. They can come to NXT to not only give back and teach the younger talent, but also to redefine and rebrand themselves before moving back to *Raw* and *SmackDown Live*.

"Tyson Kidd came back from his knee injury, and he was frustrated because the main roster had nothing for him," says Levesque. "So I asked him, 'Do you want to come down here?' He said, 'That would be great.' So I used him in NXT, and it got him noticed again. It's almost like they started watching his matches in NXT and were like, 'Oh yeah, that's right, I forgot he is pretty good. Let's start using him more on *Raw* and *SmackDown*.' Cesaro is another guy who was percolating around a little bit, so I brought him down to work with Sami Zayn, and the matches these two had made people from WWE go, 'Wow, maybe we'll put him in something bigger on *Raw*.' We weren't doing anything with Zack Ryder, so I told him about my idea to team him with Mojo Rawley. I wanted to put them together as a tag team because, with the energy they have, I can show them to Vince after they work together for a few months and he will want to bring them up. It reinvigorates Zack, and at the same time, it hides any weaknesses Mojo, a guy who we put on TV because he has a ton of charisma and energy, may have. He needs time to learn what to do, so by teaming him with a veteran, Mojo gets more experience without exposing himself. Mojo's now more relaxed in the ring because it's not all on him anymore, and he's learning a ton. Mojo is now a thousand times better because of that association and what he learned from Zack. When we can do things like that, it's great.

"Eva Marie is a perfect example. She's a victim of the *Total Divas* curse. We had just hired her before the show started; she had never trained, but E! saw her and was like, 'Wow, she has a great look. Put her on the show as a newbie just starting out.' Well, the show kept her so busy, she never got the chance to train. So the times we'd used her on TV, we kept it so simple—just showed her what to do in the moment. So she came to me and told me, 'I love *Total Divas*, but I'll quit that show tomorrow. I want to wrestle.' She really wants to do this. She's a

Bray Wyatt surveys his family's damage from his rocking chair.

jock, but she has gotten a bad rap because of the *Total Divas* thing. So I said, 'Stick with *Total Divas*, then I'll bring you to NXT and I'll retro-engineer you some street cred.' If we just train her for three months, and then put her on *Raw* or *SmackDown Live*, they will shit all over her. But if I bring her down to NXT, I can give her some street cred as she proves to the hardcore fan base that she wants this and that she's better than they think. Once she does that and the Universe believes in her, then we can move her to *SmackDown Live* and it's not such a giant risk. When she came back, they disliked her because of *Total Divas*, but she did some moves and the fans were like, 'Hey, I didn't know she could do that.' And during her second match back, they were already going back and forth with chants of 'Let's go Eva! Eva Sucks!' So there are a lot of things we can do with this brand. It's calling someone down to pitch for us for a few seasons while we teach them a new curveball before we send them back up.

"The be all and end all example of that is Bray Wyatt. Bray Wyatt was Husky Harris. When I took over Talent Development, he was sent down. Husky Harris wasn't working. He was green. We helped him come up with Bray Wyatt. He created this amazing character and persona, and before you knew it, he was working *WrestleMania* against Undertaker. He got called up, he pitched a couple of games in the Majors, he got sent back to Triple A, he revamped his entire game, and when he went back up he was closing the World Series."

Wyatt recalls his time working against veteran Superstar Chris Jericho as his favorite moment in his entire career. "Right before I started on the road, I wrestled against Chris Jericho in one of the first matches in NXT," remembers Wyatt. "That night, we shot four television shows. On the first show, I had a match and a promo. Second show, I had a promo, and the brothers (other Wyatts) had a match. Then the brothers had a match on the third show and I had a pre-tape. On the fourth show, I wrestled Jericho for 30 minutes and had a promo. It was chaos. It was really cool, and I had that moment with Jericho that I'll cherish forever. It was like Jericho welcoming me to the big leagues. I'm glad I got to share that opportunity with them."

When Samoa Joe joined NXT, he saw the emerging brand as both an opportunity and a challenge.

"A lot of guys like myself came up in an era where there were veteran guys around to give you experience," explains Joe. "During some of my first tours in Japan, I worked against some of the biggest names in the country, and just being in the ring with them and being around them really helped shape my style. They taught me certain things that you just can't learn in a classroom environment or in a ring-training environment. Hunter also came up in that type of era, and he realizes that you can't teach some things in a seminar. Sometimes, you have to be around great people to understand what makes them great, what makes them tick, to be great yourself. I think that's a big reason why Hunter chose to add me into the mix. A lot of guys like Paul Heyman and Joey Mercury vouched for me, but at the same time, he saw me as

Veteran Superstar Samoa Joe joined NXT in 2015.

a valuable key to help shape all these guys who will eventually move on to greater things."

"You are bringing in guys who have different styles and different experiences from a bunch of different places," adds Austin Aries. "That helps because you want more than just one perspective. You want to work against guys who have been all around the world and have wrestled with a bunch of different guys, different styles, and different promotions. It helps broaden their base and they may see, think, and do things differently. Obviously, the coaches are training them on the style that WWE likes to implement, but they also want to have some different perspectives. Variety is the spice of life, as they say, and it just adds a wider range of entertainment value for all the WWE Universe as well."

As for Tyler Breeze, now that he's been called up to the main roster, he can't wait to go back to NXT and pass on some of the knowledge he has learned. "NXT really started to take off, and people could see that it was starting to become a thing on its own," says Breeze. "There was *Raw*, there was *SmackDown*, but NXT was unique and people wanted to be a part of it. We had guys come down to work with us all the time. We had Rob Van Dam, Sheamus, Chris Jericho, Rhyno . . . everyone wanted to come and be a part of it. And by working with veterans like this, you're able to gain some invaluable experience. These are guys who have been working on the main roster for years, they're working on *Raw*, working on *SmackDown Live*, and now they're working with guys who are trying to get there. I think it's cool, and it's something that breathes a lot of fresh air into NXT. I know it's definitely exciting for the guys on the other end of it, like when Bray got to wrestle Jericho. That type of stuff just wasn't happening, and then all of a sudden, we're NXT and it is. It even evolved to the point where I got to wrestle Jushin 'Thunder' Liger, an international legend, in front of almost 16,000 people in Brooklyn. It was the only match that Liger's ever had in WWE, and it might be the only match he ever has in WWE, and I got to do it in front of a sold-out crowd. That was a groundbreaking moment for us. We had never worked in front of that many people

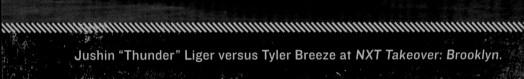

Jushin "Thunder" Liger versus Tyler Breeze at *NXT Takeover: Brooklyn*.

before. And that was all on us; we didn't have anyone to boost the sales. The fact that it worked and the fact that I got that opportunity is pretty awesome. I sat back and tried to take it all in for a moment. I went from being Mike Dalton to Tyler Breeze, a guy who was hot and who was working important matches. Getting to work with guys like Liger and Finn Bálor—huge names around the world—and becoming an essential part of NXT was really cool. As I transition my way out of there, one of the things I look forward to is being invited to come back to work with guys in NXT and to give them the experience I got when I was there. I'm also looking forward to going back just to give back to that audience. I was in front of them for so long, and they don't forget that. That's what I look forward to."

CHAPTER 11
#GiveDivasAChance

Give Divas a Chance. The Divas Revolution. Whatever you want to call the movement, there's no denying the paradigm shift that's affected women's wrestling since 2014. It's also no coincidence that 2014 was the year of *NXT Arrival*, and the introduction of Paige and Emma to the WWE Universe.

The revolution almost didn't happen. Paige, who entered development with the mindset that she was going to change the game—change the way women's wrestling was perceived—didn't even get signed when she first tried out for WWE. The woman who is now known for not conforming didn't pass her tryout because she showed up trying to play the role of a WWE Diva rather than being herself.

"My whole family wrestles, so I've been in sports entertainment my whole life," Paige says. "WWE does two tours in Europe, and I had two tryouts. During my first tryout, I did what I thought a Diva was supposed to do. I dyed my hair lighter; I got a tan. I got scouted at one of the shows, they told me to come in for a tryout, and I wrestled the way I thought a Diva should. I didn't get in because I wasn't comfortable. They gave me another opportunity when they toured in November 2010, and I decided to go as myself. I didn't care what people thought; my attitude had completely changed. I tried to be who I thought I was supposed to be and that didn't work. So I decided I to go as Saraya, which is my real name, with pale skin, black hair, my piercings in, and my all-black clothes, and if they didn't like it, they didn't like it, but at least I'd be true to myself. They loved it, which was cool. It was different from what they already had. So I got signed after the second tryout, and I started in January. They brought me into FCW.

"At that time, I was the only one who looked different. All the girls in FCW were like Summer Rae—all these gorgeous supermodels. I was something different. Something to spice it up." Some of the other women at FCW didn't appreciate the way Paige stood out, however; back then, everyone in development was fighting for the attention of the main office, and with Paige's background as a wrestler and her unique look, she shot to the top of the depth chart almost immediately.

"When I first got there, the girls weren't very nice to me," remembers Paige. "The only one who was nice to me was Summer Rae because we started at the same time. She was always super sweet. The rest of the girls—unfortunately, none of them made it to the main roster—eventually started to become nice to me, but their initial excuse was, 'You were different and you already had previous wrestling experience.' They said it was intimidating to see a girl come in like that, especially since none of them had previous wrestling experience. They all came in as models or as wrestlers' daughters, and they had to learn from scratch. I come in and I'm like, I'm already halfway there. Plus, I look different, so I stood out."

One day during training, the FCW women attempted to gang up on Paige and accused her of trying to injure Summer Rae on purpose. "There was one point when Norman Smiley, who was our trainer at the time, had me and Summer go through this wrestling move where I tackled her, we knocked shoulders, and she fell down," says Paige. "I was used to being on the indies where I would stick it in stiff but safe, where I was really snug, and she was used to dipping low because all the girls were a lot shorter than us. So I gave her this tackle, and she dipped low, not expecting me to go that hard, and her teeth went into my shoulder. She lay on the floor, crying, and this was my first week there. The other girls were like, 'She's trying to sabotage you; she's trying to get you fired,' and I'm like, 'No, I'm not. It was an accident, you crazy bitches.' They were nuts.

Paige versus Emma for the NXT Women's Championship at *NXT Arrival.*

"Even Norman called me. I was the only female who wasn't going to *WrestleMania* in Miami because I had only been there for about four months. So Norman called me, and he said, 'I just want to apologize if you thought I was mean.' Norman is not a mean person, so I didn't realize he was being mean to me, but he said, 'I'm sorry if I was ever rude or mean to you. When you first came in, I believed you thought your shit didn't stink because you were on the indies, but I was proven wrong. You're actually really nice, so I apologize for any of the trouble you went through in the first few months. Also, you're going to *Wrestle-Mania*.' So I was like, 'Oh, wow, now people can be nice to me. Now I've done the initiation.' But it's not like that anymore; it's like a big family now. In FCW, you were fighting to get attention. Now, the right people are in Orlando watching us every week. I understood why I was being treated differently, but I was like, 'Dude, I want to be here. I'll start from scratch. I'll do whatever you want just to be here.'"

For Paige, it was about having a new vision for the Women's Division. "I came into FCW thinking, 'I'm going to create change,'" she says. "That's what I always wanted to do. I wanted to be the different Diva. I'm not trying to mold myself into what a Diva is supposed to be. I'm going to be different. Eventually, there were more girls coming in with the same attitude, which was great, but it was hard because at that point in time, people were classifying the Divas as the 'toilet break.' It was really hard to overcome that and to get the respect from the WWE Universe and even from some of the guys in the business. So we were struggling with those obstacles at the time."

In 2012, two things changed the landscape of women's wrestling: Paul Levesque officially took over WWE's developmental program and told the women to go all out in their matches, and he hired legendary female grappler Sara Amato to become NXT and the Performance Center's first female coach.

"It was actually a little bit of a struggle to get hired and define what my position was," says Amato. "They didn't know what it was going to be—whether I'd be more of a player/coach, teaching the girls during

Coach Sara Amato gives valuable advice.

live events, or if I'd have my own class like all of the other coaches at the Performance Center. We just figured it out as we went. There were a lot of growing pains, and it was completely different than what I was used to, but we have a great group of girls and they all have the same passion to perform, and to do it with no limitations."

Amato says she fell in love with training new talent almost immediately and traded in her tights to become a full-time coach in Orlando.

"It's a lot less painful," she laughs, explaining that the key to developing new talent is getting to know them as individuals and tapping into what drives each of them. "All of the girls are so different, and everyone communicates and learns on a different level. We spend so much time with each other, so it's about getting to know them so you can emphasize their strong points while working on and covering up their weaker points. But really, my philosophy is just 'make it good.' Work as hard you can, produce, and stay true to you. A lot of people come here and think that we want them to do something different, but we want you to be you and be comfortable because you're going to reap the rewards. It's your image, so be you and be happy. I always say, if you're genuine, that translates—so no matter what, just be genuine."

"Those girls down in NXT, with Sara Amato as their head trainer, weren't afraid of change," says Seth Rollins. "They wanted to do something different. They wanted to showcase their athleticism to the entire world. They wanted to make everybody stand up and recognize that they could be the main event. It's gutsy enough for them to think that, but for them to go out and prove that it's possible—that can give you goosebumps. That's a special thing. That opportunity knocks but once a generation, maybe less, so for them to have the guts to stand up and say, 'This is how we're going to do things. We're going to change the game.' That's pretty incredible."

"NXT definitely provided the opportunity for all females in the company," says Paige. "Once Hunter took over, he gave the girls a chance. He said, 'If you think you can do as well as the guys, here's your opportunity.' And sometimes, the girls could do even better than the guys. Right now, the girls in NXT are main-eventing, and that blows my mind. It's incredible. They're getting 20 to 25, sometimes 30, minutes to have their match, and that's usually what the men can do. We used to get only eight minutes, or even less, on the main roster. NXT kick-started the Divas Revolution; Hunter gave us the opportunity, and the girls took that opportunity and ran with it.

"But I feel people really took a shine to it after *NXT Arrival*. People really took notice. It was a long, bumpy road. There were girls coming in and out and in and out, so it was like me and Emma carrying this on our shoulders for a little bit, trying to make it into what it is. Luckily, we had all of these awesome girls come in and help us because it was definitely hard."

The Paige-Emma match at *Arrival* was both groundbreaking and eye opening. For the first time since the glory days of Trish Stratus,

Emma takes control of Paige at *NXT Arrival*.

Lita, and Mickie James, the WWE Universe was buzzing about women in the ring, not because of what they were wearing, but because of how they were wrestling.

"I was out for three months before *NXT Arrival*," Paige remembers. "I had to have a non-wrestling related surgery, and *NXT Arrival* was coming up. So I had this massive scar around my groin area from my surgery. But there was this excitement of being on the first NXT pay-per-view, and I didn't want to mess up. This was the first time, really, people in the WWE Universe got to see us. This was the first time it was going global, so there was definitely a lot of pressure, especially for us because we were the only women on the show, and we were in a singles match. I was very thankful, but it was a ton of pressure. When we came back, they were so proud of us. That's the first time we heard 'This is awesome!' chants during a women's match, so we were so pumped. We had a great day."

Levesque was looking for a way to push the women, but at the same time, he needed them to step up for NXT's biggest moment, and that's exactly what Emma and Paige did.

"I've always felt like the Divas and our women were underutilized," says Levesque. "I felt like there was a way to position them better. A way that was more inspirational and more empowering for women. We wanted to have women's matches that a little girl or a young woman could watch and say, 'I want to do that. What they are doing inspires me.' I felt like we had created this image of the Divas that wasn't very flattering and we were limited by what we were doing. We changed that image in NXT. I remember having a conversation with Paige and Emma at *Arrival* and telling them, 'You're going to have 20 minutes,' and they looked at me like, 'What?' They were just shocked. I said, 'Do what you do. Show the world what you do . . . show them who you are.' It was never about treating them any differently; it was about treating them like the athletes they are— world-class athletes who put on amazing performances. We give the same attention to their storylines, to their rivalries, to everything as

we do the guys. We do contract signings with them, we do whatever it takes to tell that story. And then they're able to take that and do incredible things in the ring and make you believe and make you want to be more like them.

"And I think it's empowering to see what has slowly taken place here, to see how this 'Give Divas a Chance' movement has grown. Vince is running this empire and he doesn't see everything—he's aware of things, but he can't see all of it. I remember when the Give Divas a Chance thing took off; a lot of the chatter was 'Why don't they treat the women like they do at NXT?'

"He was getting all of this input from the office and he looked at me and said, 'Treat the women like they do at NXT. What do you do so different that is causing all this uproar?' I said, 'I don't do anything *different* . . . I treat them like athletes. I let them do what they do. I tell stories with them, I don't make them a side story.' And it's taken time, but this

Charlotte is ready for Sasha Banks at *NXT Takeover: R Evolution*.

whole Divas Revolution thing is one of the things I'm most proud of."

But the revolution was only beginning with Paige and Emma; waiting in the wings were Charlotte, Sasha Banks, Becky Lynch, and Bayley. The group dubbed The Four Horsewomen was about to step up and take the Women's Division to an entirely new level.

"Charlotte is a really interesting story. She was out with a foot injury early on, and she is such an amazing athlete and such a perfectionist, she'd still come to training when she was sidelined. That's when she got to step back and observe," says Amato. "When she came back from her injury, she understood so much more and was a completely different person. Sasha had a similar thing happen. She had a broken nose, so she was also able to sit back and watch for a bit, and then came back with a new determination and fire. When you're in development, it's such a full schedule—being able to take a step back really enables you to reevaluate and evolve."

"We're not just there for looks— we're here to be equal."

And they developed to the point where fans were suddenly talking about the women of NXT as equal to the men, even hoping to see the top stars in the main events of specials.

"The whole world is changing, and the number one thing that people are talking about is women in sports," says Banks. "You see that with the women's soccer team, you see that in Ronda Rousey, you see that with Hillary Clinton; you hear women are taking over. For the longest time in the WWE, women weren't given the chance to show what we can bring and we weren't treated as equals; I would watch three-minute matches with no storyline and no reason to even be in the ring. Why even have the segment if you're not gonna do anything? And I would get so frustrated because we were given so much time here in NXT and we worked for that, so I was like, 'How does that not happen up there? What's going on? What are they missing?' I think people have been waiting for a change. They want something different. They want to see what the NXT women can do, and they want to see that on the main roster; they want to watch every single week, and they want to watch women do what they know they can do for more than a three-minute segment. Ever since we made our debut on the main roster and the Divas Revolution, we've had Divas on *Raw* every week for matches longer than three

minutes, longer than five minutes, longer than eight minutes, and the response is amazing. I came back from a match against Paige, and Vince stood up and shook my hand. Paige told me that he never does that, so that just tells you that there's a change happening. I know this is only the beginning for women. I have dreams of main-eventing *Raw*, and I want people to watch the pay-per-view just to see my match. I think that's going to happen because I see myself as equal to the men, and I think the WWE Universe is starting to see that too. We're not just Divas, we're not just there for looks—we're here to be equal."

In NXT, Levesque didn't even want the women to be known as Divas, a precursor of what was to come in WWE months later. "We're

Triple H congratulates Bayley at *NXT Takeover: Respect*.

not calling them Divas down here. Paul likes it that way," says Canyon Ceman. "But I want to take a step back and talk about what I think is a big turning point in the history of this brand and maybe the industry: hiring Sara Amato as the first female trainer for the women. She came in and really put her imprint on the division and taught them how to construct matches. She taught them how to move in the way that she is the best on the planet at. When I think of the history of NXT, she's an important piece because with Paul's guidance and empowerment and booking style, she made these women more than they had been and that was a differentiator for the brand. The strength, the professionalism, the empowerment of the female talent made NXT different than *Raw*, and I think a big part of our audience really appreciated that. Some of those early Charlotte versus Natalya matches and the Emma versus Paige match became big inflection points in the history of this brand and contributed to the Give Divas a Chance story that has become part of the company. Right now, we are seeing it change the game in real time. We always say, 'You ladies are changing the game,' and Sara Amato changed the game, and Triple H changed the game by giving Sara and the women time to tell their stories, empowering them, and now you're seeing the results on *Raw*. They truly are changing the game."

The women who entered WWE Development and led this charge for change accomplished it by working towards their common goal together, both in and out of the ring. Instead of bickering over who won the Championship or who was going to be called up first, the women of NXT used teamwork and friendship to gain the respect of the WWE Universe.

"When I came back from my tryout, I said to my friend, 'I'm going to main event *WrestleMania* one day,' and he said, 'You know, it's nice to dream, but you've got to be realistic,'" Becky Lynch remembers. "I said, 'Just watch me. One day we will; we're going to main event.' I want women's wrestling to be seen as really, really cool, and to be as respected as the men's because why not? We're all people, right? And it doesn't matter whether you're male or female. We're all equal, and if you're going to put in the hard work, then you should get the same rewards. There's a global shift in how women are being viewed, and that is true of WWE. This is what I've always wanted. It's like I had this dream as a little girl, and as a woman it's become a vision, and this vision is getting clearer and clearer every day.

"The thing about the Four Horsewomen is that every one of them, Charlotte, Sasha, and Bayley, is at the top of her game. They are incredible athletes, incredible characters, and incredible performers. So you can't rest on your laurels because as soon as you do, somebody is going to get better than you. You're always competing. Not necessarily

The Four Horsewomen (left to right): Becky Lynch, Bayley, Charlotte, and Sasha Banks.

against them but against yourself—because you constantly want to be better than you were before, because they are constantly getting better than they were before, because of everybody constantly growing and constantly getting better. We all get better because nobody wants to get left behind. I think that's the best part about it and what is so wonderful. Yeah, we all want to be the best; absolutely every single one of us wants to be the best. And in a way, we all are because we are all so different. I am competing against Sasha or I'm competing against Charlotte or I'm competing against Bayley, but it's not in the same way because I'm not in any way like them and they're in no way like me. We all drive each other to be the best versions of ourselves, and that's the best kind of competition because we're not comparing ourselves to anybody. But we can constantly work to be better than we were before.

"It's unbelievable because as much as we work for this and as much as this has been a vision for all of us, it's been Triple H's vision, and we can't do it without him giving us the opportunity and without him believing in us and supporting us and showing us that faith. We feel like little kids that are making their dad proud. He really has taken us under his wing and really believes in us and takes the time to talk to us and cares about where the direction of women's wrestling is going. Maybe it's because he has three daughters. He's a remarkable boss and a remarkable human being. It's incredible to know that we all have the same vision. It's also really cool because I was such a fan of his when I was a teenager—I knew him as The Game—and having him be proud of what we're doing is such a dream come true. I always pinch myself—how did this little girl from Dublin, Ireland, get here? We're building this thing that the world has never seen . . . we're making history. It's amazing."

"Our female performers are Superstars by any definition of the word," says Stephanie McMahon, WWE's Chief Brand Officer. "For them to have the opportunity to succeed and earn the same respect as their male counterparts is extremely important for WWE. What we've called the Divas Revolution is actually part of a larger revolution

Above: Bayley with a suplex on rival Charlotte.
Right: Charlotte versus Sasha Banks at *NXT Takeover: R Evolution*.

happening throughout sports and entertainment. You look at the success of Ronda Rousey, Venus and Serena Williams, the U.S. Women's Soccer Team, and so many other inspiring women, and you wonder, 'Why shouldn't our female performers have the same opportunity in WWE?' Not only are they world-class athletes, they are actors, public speakers, philanthropists, and role models. They inspire women and girls all over the world to be confident and strong.

"And the WWE Universe demanded that our female performers be given this spotlight when they started a hashtag on Twitter called #GiveDivasAChance. It trended worldwide for three days. The message was one of empowerment; it was a cry for WWE to have more character development and feature our women in more prominent storylines and longer matches, giving them the platform to showcase their incredible talents. This movement was so important that our Chairman & CEO, Vince McMahon, responded personally on Twitter: 'We hear you, keep watching. #GiveDivasAChance.'"

From Charlotte versus Natalya to the Fatal 4-Way between The Four Horsewomen to Banks and Charlotte main-eventing NXT to Bayley and Sasha bringing down the house in Brooklyn, the women in NXT keep building on their reputation, and the WWE Universe can't get enough.

"I think the biggest thing that we share is our love for this industry, and because we were fans first, we understand what the fans want," says Banks. "We wanted to be like the guys. We wanted to have these long matches, and we would train every single day with each other so we could get to know each other. And we created these matches in NXT that were just so magical, I can't describe it. People would come up to talk to us and we just connected with the WWE Universe over this magic that was in the ring. Of course, everyone's dream is to make it to the main roster, to be on *Raw* and *SmackDown Live* and the pay-per-views and *WrestleMania*, but we have it so good here. We were given the chance and we took the ball and we rolled with it. But we didn't want to give that up for three-minute matches, so I think we all just kind of united for a change. We needed a change for the future of this business. We want what we have in NXT on the main roster, so we have to stay connected, we have to look out for each other, and we have to be close because that's what makes our matches so special.

"We are so close and we're willing to give our bodies to each other to create these magical matches for years to come. We want the WWE Universe to talk about how much they enjoy our matches and how they want to see the women's match in the main event and that they paid to see us. It feels so good to be given the opportunities and to be a part of history. I got to main event with Charlotte in front of thousands at the NXT Philly show, and I remember freaking out when they told me because I was like, 'Why me? Why? You have Finn Bálor, you have Kevin Owens, you have all this incredible, incredible talent, but you chose me? Charlotte and me to main event? In front of a Philly crowd? Like, are you guys crazy?' So I just remember crying and crying. I came back from that match and all the fans were standing on their feet, no one left, and that feeling is the feeling that I live for; once you experi-

Future *SmackDown* Women's Champion Becky Lynch in NXT.

ence that, you can't go back. It's what drives me to keep striving for more and more."

To Charlotte and Bayley, the ability to strive for more begins and ends with the woman who pushed them to strive for more in the first place, Sara Amato.

"To me, the biggest difference in how we're training women compared to anywhere around the world is Sara Amato," says Charlotte. "She has trained and wrestled all over the world, and she has the ability to take people from the independents and from all different backgrounds—people who have never even wrestled before—and teach them the right way to do everything in and out of the ring. We not only have the seven rings and the weight room and the promo room, but we also have a secret weapon, and that's Sara."

"When I first got here, the main thing I was excited for was being able to train with Sara Amato," says Bayley. "Before I was even signed, I

Bayley and Sasha Banks embrace after a 30-minute Iron Man match.

was trying to train with her and to have matches with her, so to be able to work with her in the Performance Center was like a dream come true. Then, when I saw she was training the women just like how the guys were being trained, I was blown away. We were working just as hard as the guys, going through the same drills and learning the same moves. What I really noticed at first was that I needed to train for the camera. First, it was training so I could wrestle, then it was training so I could do it in front of a crowd, but what Sara taught us was how to work in front of the camera. She taught us how to face the camera in order to really show off specific moves. Things really took off when we got to the Performance Center because we filmed all of our training sessions. It's different watching yourself train as opposed to watching your matches. You can really pick up on little things. We're taking women from all levels of wrestling. There are women who come here who have never wrestled a day in their life, so being able to work with people of all different levels of talent and with people from all across the world helps make everyone better. We're really one big family at NXT. We spend at least five hours a day together, and being able to work with Sara at the Performance Center is more than I ever could've expected.

"The Divas Revolution is something that every woman wants to see continue. Every woman who enters WWE wants the WWE Universe to see us as strong women who can put on a hell of a match. We want to be looked at just like the guys. Triple H gave us that opportunity. He put these matches on whether there was a story behind it or not, and he gave us the opportunity to go out and prove ourselves. We weren't limited to five-minute matches. He gave us 10 minutes, he gave us 15 minutes, and then he just kept adding more. The more opportunities he gave us, the more we took advantage of it, and we delivered. And I'm not saying it was because of us. Triple H gave us the green light and said, 'Show us what you can do.' I don't think the girls on *Raw* were ever really given the opportunity to shine until the NXT girls got called up. But now, all of the women on *Raw* are able to show what they've got. It's good for everybody. It's amazing to see. It's something I always dreamed of as a kid, to see women highlighted so well in sports entertainment."

And with Charlotte, Sasha, and Becky all getting called up to the main roster at the same time, Levesque wants to make sure that nobody is forgetting Bayley's importance, not only to NXT, but to the women's movement as a whole.

"I feel Bayley gets left out of the equation, but she's a huge piece of it." says Levesque. "There's Charlotte, this unbelievably gifted second-generation athlete. Then there's Sasha Banks, this little spitfire who you think doesn't work on paper, she's so little, but you forget about that when she starts going. Becky is another one who came on all of a sudden. She went from kind of being there to becoming a Superstar, and all that credit goes to her. We gave her some freedom with her character, then gave her the ball and, boy, did she run with it. It's amazing to see where all of them started and where they got to, and

while I'm so proud of the revolution NXT started, all the credit has to go to the performers.

"But what's funny is, Bayley is the contradiction to every conversation about what we're looking for in a female Superstar that we'd had in the past 10 years. But that's exactly why I brought her in. I feel like she can be something more; she can inspire little girls who can't relate to the other women and who think to themselves, 'I'm never going to be that because that's just not who I am as a person.' Yet, here's Bayley; she might not be cut from the same cloth as 'the model' or have a certain 'physique type' or any of those things that would've been exactly what you painted our women to be, but she worked hard. She aspired to be more. She believed in herself and did it. If that's not inspirational to young girls, what is? And I think that she's continuing on that journey.

"I think five or 10 years from now, we're going to look back and say, 'Remember when women in WWE used to be that?' And then all of a sudden they became this whole other brand, they became inspirational and it's one of the things I'm proudest of NXT for. I think it's a change that you see across the genre of sports and entertainment. You see women superheroes in movies now and female athletes treated as legitimate athletes. It's a paradigm shift in how people perceive women in the world, in athletics, in entertainment, in business, in everything. It's awesome, and if we were any tiny bit a part of that, that's awesome. Now, it's about keeping that momentum going. Fans can say, 'Yeah, NXT was on fire because they had Charlotte and Sasha and Becky, but now they're all gone. How are they going to top it?' When the stars get called up, is NXT doomed? No. We reinvigorated the Divas division on *Raw* with four girls. If we can't make four more girls in NXT, something's wrong with us. It's creating new talent, it's finding new talent—that's part of the charm of NXT. Hopefully, they'll all continue to go away, so we're constantly working to build new stars.

"Charlotte even said it in an interview recently, 'I don't see any limits. One day women will headline *WrestleMania*.' When they started,

"I don't see any limits. One day women will headline WrestleMania."

I told them they could do anything. It's not, 'You're a Diva, you can only do this or you can only do that.' We have fostered them in a way that shows they can do and accomplish anything. The fact that there is a Divas Revolution, the fact that those girls got called up and it led to longer matches on *Raw*, and the way the WWE Universe is reacting to them as a whole just goes to show that the acceptance is there. There are some people who are kicking and screaming, but it's a shift in opinion and attitude that takes time. It's not like all of a sudden it's different, but it's getting there. Five years ago, you'd never imagine that a female would be headlining a UFC pay-per-view or that Ronda Rousey would be the hottest athlete on the planet. You would also never have said that three girls would come to WWE and change the face of the division. If I showed you Sasha, Charlotte, and Becky Lynch, not to mention Bayley, on paper, you would have said, 'You're out of your mind.' But here we are. I think whether it takes time or whether it's quick, we're open to what the WWE Universe wants. If they want women to headline *WrestleMania*, it will happen. It just takes time."

Stephanie McMahon sees in The Four Horsewomen the talent to overcome any odds, and she truly does expect to see them headlining a *WrestleMania* in the near future. "Just like those who came be-

The Four Horsewomen unite to celebrate Bayley and Sasha's epic performance.

fore them—dating all the way back to Fabulous Moolah, the Great Mae Young, Luna Vachon, Sherri Martel, Hall of Famers Jacqueline, Alundra Blayze, Lita, and Trish, and current stars Paige, The Bellas, Natalya, and Naomi to name a few—The Four Horsewomen have an undeniable charisma and unrivaled athleticism that is captivating to our audience. Go back and watch the historic Triple Threat Match for the inaugural WWE Women's Championship at *WrestleMania 32*. Charlotte, Becky Lynch, and Sasha Banks, all in their first year on the main roster, were able to deliver a performance for the ages in front of a record crowd of more than 100,000 fans. To be able to deliver in such a fashion, in such a high-pressure spot, should tell you that these are special performers who will not be ignored. If given the opportunity to one day main-event *WrestleMania*, I have no doubt they will over-deliver and steal the show."

"NXT has been able to develop really strong female athletes," adds Alexa Bliss. "We give the women a very strong image, and I think it's awesome that WWE and NXT women are able to work together and bring this Revolution to life. It's what we've been wanting. We can work. We can wrestle. We can do it."

"I take pride in the Divas Revolution," says Paige as she smiles, thinking back about her matches that started it all. "It's been dubbed the Divas Revolution now, but back then, Emma and I just wanted change. People backed us up and gave us that voice, so we're definitely very, very, very proud. I'm one of the youngest, but I'm like the momma bear. I'm super proud of them. I don't want it to be ruined. If someone ruins it, they're in so much trouble."

But to Stephanie McMahon, the Divas Revolution is just the first step to something bigger as she works with the company to rebrand the Divas Division to the Women's Division. "We branded the division 'Divas' beginning in 2008 in an effort to give our female performers a more prominent role," she explains. "The Divas Division launched several successful careers and led to the creation of the wildly popular reality show on E! called *Total Divas*.

"But the WWE Universe wanted more. The Divas Revolution started an evolution, and it only made sense for us to debut the new Women's Division with the new Championship on our biggest stage, *WrestleMania*. I thought Lita said it best when she presented the new Championship, speaking so highly of pioneers such as Fabulous Moolah, Sensational Sherri, Trish Stratus, and others. For them, it wasn't about gender, race, or ethnicity. It was simply about being the best at what you do. That is what WWE is all about."

CHAPTER 12
Less Talk, More Action

When discussing NXT's success, everyone from Levesque to the talent themselves talk about one thing: WWE Network. But it's not simply airing on the Network that has keyed NXT's meteoric rise, it's the type of show they're promoting, from the conflicts inside the ring to even the amount of time they're on air. One taped hour per week, with four specials a year. No overexposure. No time for long-winded rants in the ring. Just down and dirty action that plays out more like ECW or *Ring of Honor* than *Raw*.

"I feel like what NXT brings is something completely opposite of what you see on *Raw* and *SmackDown Live*," says Sasha Banks. "It's like this underground layer of WWE that no one *should* know about but everybody *wants* to know about. We have talent from all over the world and I think that's what makes it really special. Not one person here is the same. Everyone comes from a different background, everyone has a different story, everyone's here for a different reason, but for the same reason too—to be the best and to have incredible matches. I'm a fan of NXT. I love watching it. My favorite men are Tyler Breeze and Sami Zayn. The matches they bring to the table are incredible. It's something you don't see on *Raw* or *SmackDown Live*. We have this excitement; we have this buzz about us. Everyone wants to know what NXT is, and you really have to be here to see it and to feel it—people love it. We're really taking over the world."

"You're seeing the influx of guys on *Raw* and *SmackDown Live* who are coming from NXT and who were originally in the independents,

and you're seeing the wrestling style on TV change due to them," adds Cesaro. "When you see new performers who have a different style . . . that's the beauty of this art. Everyone is unique. I think there is also a one-upmanship on the main roster and down in NXT. If one of the people I hang out with has a great match, I want to have a better one. If I have a good match, they want to have a better one than me. There are a lot of eyes on NXT, and that can be a positive, but that can also be a negative. When you're brand new, it's not good to be in the spotlight right away, because you're not ready for it, but with NXT, it's sink or swim."

Paul Levesque agrees that the non-stop action and unique styles are key, but he also knows that part of NXT's early success is being "the new kid in town."

"A year from now we are not going to be the shiny new penny," he says. "We'll have been here awhile and we'll be established. It's great to drive a new car, it's awesome. How much do you love that car when you're still driving it around a year from now and you've been driving

it around every day? You have to keep them excited, you have to keep them engaged and you have to keep it fresh. That's the challenge. What makes the WWE Universe spread the word and what makes them want to come back? To me, it's just giving them great storylines. It's no different than what works for WWE or for the main roster or for *Raw* and *SmackDown Live* or anything else. In this case, the stories can be more concise because we're kind of going after a particular group. We want good stories, good rivalries, great delivery of matches, and to create an exciting environment where even predictable is unpredictable. And I think that is the trick of what we do because not letting it be predictable is the real challenge. Kevin Owens is on the main roster,

Triple H gives Neville some post-match encouragement.

Sasha Banks is on the main roster—so is what they're doing on NXT now predictable? We'll make sure it's not predictable.

"We want to engage the WWE Universe in something they think is awesome no matter what, whether it's an individual talent, whether it's the overall product, or whether it's just a feeling they get when they watch. It makes you want to talk about it. With NXT, one of the other important things is that it's a one-hour weekly show. It's a two-hour live event special. It's quick and it's fast and we don't take our foot off the pedal. We step on the gas, we go straight through two hours, and you're wiped out when you're done watching. You're like, 'Oh my God, that was amazing.' There was never a let up, there was never a dull point, there was never anything that sort of slowed down and made you think, 'Okay, I can sit down now before the main event comes on.' There's a charm to that. It's different, so it feels cool. We just want to make people excited, and if we can make them excited enough to go and tell their friends about it, even better."

Part of that is taking the creative in unique and different directions, but with a development brand and working with development talent, Levesque says that you actually can't plan too far in advance—he doesn't know when someone will get called up until he gets the fateful message from Stamford. So while Levesque and the creative team like to plan out a few months in advance where characters might be headed, a lot can change between the time something gets put on paper and when someone is actually headed to the ring for a taped show.

"I remember when Kevin Owens got called up, I was like, 'Fuck! He's in the middle of a rivalry with Finn!' But you just have to roll with it," says Levesque. "It's just one of the challenges of putting on a TV show."

Another important challenge of teaching performers in development: how to perform moves for the camera.

"WWE matches are televised, so being taught the camera angles is as important as learning to take bumps and the different techniques you perform in the ring," says Neville. "It's all a part of what we do,

and the way they teach it in NXT just gives you such an advantage for when you appear on *Raw*. You already know how the camera is going to capture your moves, you already know how to walk down the ramp because everything you do in NXT is repeated on *Raw*, just in front of more people."

Neville also credits the NXT creative team with developing some of the best characters in the industry.

"NXT is huge in helping establish your character," he says. "The environment in the Performance Center is very positive, and the creativity in the building is infectious. There are so many cool characters that are being created in NXT; it really is an exciting place to be."

Apollo Crews sees his character as a work in progress, but he loves the ability to approach creative with ideas.

"If somebody has an idea, they can pitch it to creative, and if creative has an idea for you, they'll approach you about it," says Crews. "Maybe you can work on your ideas together and meet somewhere in the middle. A lot of it is on us. We can't just sit around and wait for something to come to us. It's always a good idea to be working on new ideas. It's like working outside of work. You're thinking of ideas and writing them down. Being able to relay those ideas to the creative team or to someone who can get it into the creative team's hands is just so important. I think that's where a lot of guys get stuck. They don't work outside of work. I admit I need to work harder to come up with ideas that I can pitch so I'm always evolving, so I'm always changing, and I never get stuck standing still. I'm a go-with-the-flow guy. I don't want to know too far in advance because so many things can change in that time that can alter what's going on, so you have to be able to adapt to any situation. Even when you're going out to the ring and you're in that moment, something can change and you need to be able to adapt."

Finn Bálor actually holds the opposite position; leaving creative decisions to the writing team means more time for him to fine-tune his character and moves.

"I'm sure some people love to put in their two cents, but I just like

The Demon King makes his entrance as NXT Champion.

Sami Zayn's explosive offense on display in NXT.

to worry about myself," says Bálor. "It's not my job to take care of storylines; that's somebody else's job. I'm just going to show up to work and make the most out of whatever they want me to do. Any type of storyline I would come up with would be from only my perspective, and I'm sure the writing team and the creative team assess their stories from all points of view. I trust them; that's their job. My job is to take that storyline and play it out the best way that I can."

As for talent getting called up in the middle of rivalries, Bálor actually sees NXT as a victim of its own success. "Maybe NXT wasn't supposed to be as successful as it is now, and maybe people getting called up in the past didn't affect the show, but perhaps now, people getting called up will really change storylines," he says. "As far as I'm concerned, the way NXT is going right now, I don't see the call-up as the only way to define success. NXT has its finger on the pulse of what's cool right now. It's all anyone is talking about, and I want to

> **"This is a time that's going to change the future of the business."**

be a part of it. I don't want to be the person who gets called up and then misses out on this incredible time in the business. I believe NXT is going to revolutionize the business—not only what goes on inside the ring, but how it's consumed. It's only on the network, it's not on TV, so it's a very different time, and what we're doing is something fresh and unique. I think when you look back at this time 10 years from now, you're going to see a huge point in the history of this industry. This is a time that's going to change the future of the business.

"I think it's a perfect storm that makes it great TV. It's quality in-ring product. Adrian Neville, Sami Zayn, and Cesaro led the way before us, and then the so-called indie darlings like myself and Kevin Owens joined, and we brought a lot of eyes to the product, and so do the fresh faces who are coming through the Performance Center, like Jason Jordan and Chad Gable, Dash and Dawson, Enzo and Big Cass. So you've got recognizable names who have been around a long time, you've got fresh talent coming in, you have the best storylines, the best lighting, the best camera angles, the best entrances, and the most attention to detail. I also think a huge bonus is it's not overexposed. It's only an hour a week, and it leaves people wanting more, which is a huge component of its success."

But as NXT gains viewers, don't expect Bálor to be one of them. "You may be surprised to hear this, but I don't go online much," he says. "I don't watch the product. I don't watch WWE Network because I'd like my perspective to remain my perspective and not be influenced by a third party. I'm experiencing NXT through my point of view and that's all I need to know as a performer. I don't need to see the other end of it because I don't want to change anything I'm doing. The way I see it, NXT is the coolest thing in our industry right now, and that's the only thing I need to know. That's my opinion, and I don't need anyone else's. I don't know if that makes me an egomaniac, but that's just how I want it. I want to see NXT how I see it, and I don't want to be swayed by other people."

And while Bálor might not be in the ratings' demographic, former NXT and WWE Champion Seth Rollins definitely is. Rollins loves NXT's television model, not to mention the lack of outside influences attempting to dictate the show's content. "NXT is just a different animal," he says. "They don't do live television. They do the quarterly specials that are live, but they follow the old WWE model where they essentially have four big pay-per-views per year and they tape their television. They have the ability to have a little bit of foresight in that sense, where as we do our television live every single week—the advertising on it is wild and there are all sorts of outside influences that people just don't understand. They just think, 'Oh, it's a three-hour entertainment show,' but it's so much more than that. There are so many different cooks in the kitchen and everybody has their own spices that they want to throw into the recipe, and it doesn't always work out. A lot of times, we just don't have the time or the resources to make the changes, so it's one of those things where you have to maximize your minutes. Do what you can with the time allotted. So the reason the women have gotten the short end of the stick throughout the years is because that was the formula that worked. To stray away from that is difficult. In NXT, we don't have all of this pressure coming from outside sources. It's very grassroots in that it's just the fans and the performers—that's

Seth Rollins celebrates his win in the NXT Championship Gold Rush Tournament.

it. It doesn't have all that corporate mumbo jumbo behind it just yet. I say 'just yet' because you never know when it will reach that point. But for now, it's still very raw and very real. It's just a bunch of kids with a passion for what we do who have the opportunity to go out there and artistically express how they feel about a certain story, how they feel about life, how they feel about a match. The fans are also a huge part of that. The crowd at Full Sail has become their own thing. And that energy . . . they feed off the performers, the performers feed off of them, and it has created a very awesome environment that's conducive for growth from an artistic standpoint."

Rollins also credits the internet for NXT's success. "Ten years ago, the internet fan was a small demographic; but in 2015, the kids grow

Samoa Joe and Finn Bálor continue their brutal rivalry.

up with the internet. If a fan wants to know something about Sasha Banks, they just Google it and in two seconds they have all the information they would ever need: who she's affiliated with, who she is dating, and everything else they've ever wanted to know. That's not just a casual fan, that's anybody who turns on a TV. If somebody sees me on *Good Morning America* or *The Today Show* or ESPN and they don't know who I am, the first thing they're going to do if they're interested in what I'm saying is Google Seth Rollins, and they're going to find out every single thing about me. We talk about not catering to the internet fans, but the entire WWE Universe exists on the internet. Now we're pushing our audience toward Twitter, toward Facebook, toward social media, and we're inviting them into that world. It's almost like we're peeling back the curtain another layer, similar to the way The Kliq did it way back in the 1990s. We're entering this revolution where entertainment is being consumed on so many different levels, and we have yet to fully harness that energy we've created. But there's something brewing and changing about the way people watch WWE and what they want to see from this art form. It's very interesting, and it doesn't surprise me at all that there were 15,000 people in New York City who went to watch NXT. They all want to be a part of that. It just looks like so much fun, so why would they not want to do the same thing. That's just how things are shifting, and you see that more and more."

The rise of the internet fan also enabled NXT to attempt something unique to the business: a Championship change at a non-televised show. On April 21, 2016, Samoa Joe defeated Finn Bálor in Lowell, Massachusetts, to win the NXT Championship. The win not only ended Bálor's NXT-record 292-day Championship reign, but it also proved that you don't need to change Championships at a pay-per-view special to create buzz throughout the world.

"The general idea was I would win the Championship at some point, but the decision to do it at a house show was really a conscious decision to reward our live-event crowds," says Samoa Joe. "NXT has grown beyond the perception of just a development brand and has transformed into another brand unto itself. The biggest reason that has happened is because no matter where we go, from around the U.S. to the UK, our house shows are amazing. The energy and the vibe that the fans bring to these shows is unparalleled, so the decision was made to give these fans something that's special, unique, and might never be replicated again. I think that was the thought process behind the decision.

"There is a lot of trial and error in NXT. There are certain things that you don't want to gamble on with the main roster, but you can take those chances in NXT. Winning the Championship on a house show proves just how much the landscape of entertainment has changed. When I won in Lowell, Massachusetts, people were like, 'Oh,

"It's quick and it's fast and we don't take our foot off the pedal."

that's horrible! I didn't get to see it on TV.' But these were the same people who read the thousands of tweets from fans who were there live, and then they retweeted it and watched the video of the match, which spread virally. In reality, it was probably seen by just as many people online, if not more, than if we did it only on TV. If you want to see what happened in the match, it's just a click away. And that was thought about and planned. We knew that if we did this at a house show, the internet would go crazy. Videos are going to get out there. It's like this lost footage that you're not supposed to see, but everybody is watching, and it made the fan reactions caught on cell phone cameras that much cooler. If you did this in the '80s or early '90s, it wouldn't have gotten seen until television. We did it, and it was online minutes later. It's about having your finger on the pulse of the modern media markets, and that's what NXT is all about. We continue to push the boundaries of entertainment."

"With NXT, there's a lot less talking and a lot more action," adds Paige. "It has that independent feel. It has that 'it' factor. We tell good stories with less talking. It's not like a soap opera; it's action packed. It's like an addiction: once you see one show, you want to carry on and keep watching."

CHAPTER 13
Spell It Out for Ya

In FCW, the real competition was to get out of development hell the quickest. In NXT, it's about making development better, one-upping the match before you, and even trying to one-up the main roster.

"It's very competitive, but it's not competitive to the point where people will take immoral measures to get ahead," says Big Cass. "Everybody wants to go out there and put on the best match. You return through the curtain, and it's like, 'Follow that!' But deep down, we are all rooting for each other, especially when we see one of us debuting on the main roster. When Neville debuted and when Kevin debuted, we were happy for them, but at the same time, we wanted to be in that same position. It's like a brotherhood and sisterhood at NXT. It really is a family atmosphere. Everybody wants to be the best, but when it comes down to it, only one person can be the very best."

"This is a competitive business," agrees Baron Corbin. "In anything athletic and performance based, you have to be a little selfish and competitive. It's good for the business to have the best guys bring their best game every time; so you want to out-do people, you want to out-shine people, but there's no malice to it. It's a very competitive environment, and we're grown men who are doing something that not a lot of people in this world are able to do. It's a very small funnel to get to that next level, and we're all fighting and scratching our way through that. Everybody here has a lot of pride for what NXT has become, and I think that's where the family atmosphere has come from. We built this and this is my home, and I'm not going to let anything happen to my

Baron Corbin applies a nerve hold on Austin Aries.

home. But at the end of the day, I want to be WWE Champion. We're protective and competitive.

"You have young, hungry kids here with the intent, written or unwritten, to take those top spots on the main roster," explains Terry Taylor, who on a daily basis drills into his students that they need to be competitive in order to survive the business. "Competition is good for everybody. I tell them all the time, 'There's going to be a main event in *WrestleMania* next year and the year after that and the year after that. Somebody is going to be in that spot. Why not you?' If they don't come out of here and ask, 'Why not me?' I'm not doing my job."

Enzo Amore gains notoriety for his gift of gab.

"At the end of the day, we all want to be on the WWE screen" adds Enzo Amore. "To have the opportunity to work at *WrestleMania* is why we are in this business. I try not to think too far ahead and only concern myself with today. We have work to do, and you never stop learning in this business. Fortunately for us, the Performance Center helps us learn at a pace that's never been possible before. What we're doing in this business has never been done before. The opportunity to learn at NXT is greater than it has ever been in the history of this industry. So I just try to embrace the day and the work and the time that we get to put in. I was once told by a guy on the main roster, 'Never let this place use you; learn to use it.' Sometimes, when you walk through the doors of the Performance Center, it's like Groundhog Day—you get into the ring and you get your butt kicked and you get thrown around, and you lift weights and it's the same workout as last Monday and your hips hurt, and now you're cutting a promo and you're standing in the mirror—and it becomes monotonous. But that's what we live to do. So taking it day by day and using it to your advantage is the ultimate way to embrace your dreams. If you want to be on the WWE main roster, there's more opportunity to do it now than there's ever been before. In the next five years, I think that you will see a better product than you've ever seen before. NXT became a brand for a reason; it's not merely developmental. In the years to come, everyone that you see in WWE will have come from NXT and will have trained under the watchful eye of WWE trainers who want their product to be a certain way and who want the WWE Universe to enjoy it. On a grander scale, what we're doing is going to be monumental in the history of sports-entertainment. What we do is going to be revolutionary."

Sami Zayn loves the competition, but he's competing to be the best he can be. He doesn't worry about other people on the roster. "Maybe it's for my own sanity, but I'm of the belief that the competition within NXT is more with yourself than the guy next to you," Zayn explains. "As far as I'm concerned, there's only one of me, and there's only one of you, so we're not both competing for the Sami Zayn spot. Only I can have the

Kevin versus Sami Zayn at *NXT Takeover: Arrival.*

Sami Zayn spot, because I'm Sami Zayn. Just like I can't compete for the Finn Bálor spot, because he's Finn Bálor. So the best thing you can do is be the best you and create your own spot and leave a void when you're gone. There is a certain level of competition because there are a couple of people in that bullpen position who are ready to go up any day now, they're just waiting for the right time. I'm a big believer that things will happen when they're supposed to happen, and to get there is more of a competition with myself than with the guys sitting next to me."

At the same time, he does see the crowd starting to take sides between *Raw* and NXT. "It's very funny how WWE is now running the hottest indie promotion. It's kind of crazy because NXT feels like the old ECW," says Zayn. "It has an anti-establishment feeling while actually being part of the establishment, so it's a very unique promotion. It's an alternative to the company within the company. When we did our first NXT shows outside of Florida, we were in Columbus and Cleveland. Unfortunately, I was injured at the time, so I went out there to cut a promo and do an interview, and the crowd was chanting, 'Better than *Raw*! Better than *Raw*!' It was almost like an outcry for something fresh, and that's why they've gravitated toward NXT. There's a little bit of angst in there, there's hostility, but they're supporting the same company, so it's funny.

"I think any time anyone is on a different side of the fence than somebody else, there are going to be some weird battle lines that are drawn, even if they are not serious. I think a lot of us in NXT have the mentality that we're just as good as anybody on the main roster, and once we get to the main roster, we're going to prove it. At the same time, I'm sure everybody on the main roster hears all this buzz about the NXT roster, and they're thinking, 'We'll show them.' That's a healthy level of competition, in my opinion, but again, we're all pulling for the same company at the end of the day. Competition makes everyone better, and that's what drives products forward. I don't think it's a bad thing."

And according to Cesaro, the crowd chanting for NXT is not lost on the main roster.

"What we do is going to be revolutionary."

"We are all going to try and one-up anything we see," he says. "When NXT was at the Barclays Center with *SummerSlam*, there was a vibe from both rosters of 'Let's show them how it's done.'"

Samoa Joe agrees, "The competition between NXT and the main roster is an absolutely conscious thing. When we do a special right before a major WWE pay-per-view, that's a gauntlet being thrown. We're telling the world—we're telling the main roster—this is what we can do, now follow that. I think it's a healthy challenge for guys on the main roster. It just gives them more motivation to go out and wreck it. I think all of the great grapplers, entertainers, and performers of our time always love a little competition on their heels, and if we can provide that and inject a little inspiration into their performance for the night, so be it. As long as NXT is pushing like that, all it's going to do is make everybody better."

Head Coach Matt Bloom understands that the competition inside the Performance Center also helps push talent to improve at a rapid rate. "We have three-day tryout camps, and there are some people who come in here who cannot do a somersault, and by day three, they are learning how to control their body and are a lot more agile than they were when they came in," says Bloom. "When some of the talent first arrived, I was worried they might hurt themselves or someone else. But those guys are quality entertainers now, and some of them will be on the roster soon.

"People are developing into Superstars. When Baron Corbin came from the NFL, he was athletic, he could move and controlled his body well, but when he stepped into the ring, he just used to beat people and beat people. You need to have controlled aggression. He never had to control his aggression before; here's the guy in front of you, knock off his helmet and take him out of the game because the guy behind him is a lot easier. That was Baron Corbin. He's a big, aggressive guy, so learning how to do what we do was a little bit more difficult for him, but now he's pretty damn good at what he does. Then there's someone like Braun Strowman, a powerlifter who can lift the world for one rep.

But he's not in the ring for one or two minutes; he's going to be in there for 10 or 15 minutes. So again, here is someone who couldn't control his own body at first, but now he's this big 6-foot-8, 385-pound man who's pretty damn agile.

"If you ask me, the competition inside the Performance Center is one of the main things that drives its success."

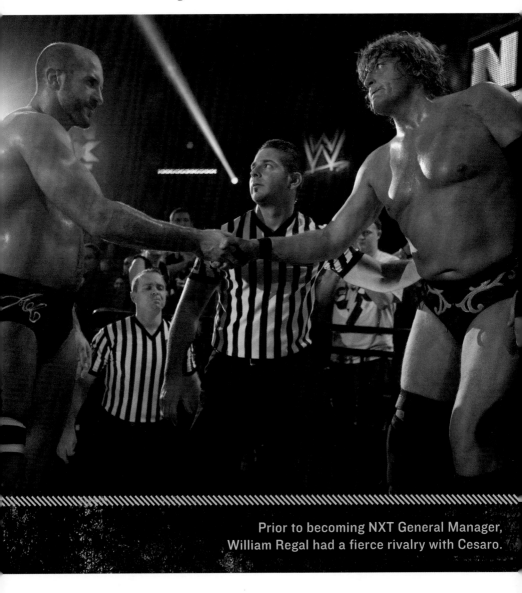

Prior to becoming NXT General Manager, William Regal had a fierce rivalry with Cesaro.

CHAPTER 14
Realest Guy in the Room

It's hours before an NXT taping, and Paul Levesque is inside the ring with Finn Bálor and Kevin Owens, going over every moment of the heated confrontation they are going to have in the show later on. For a good five minutes, Levesque picks up a ladder from inside the ring and shows Bálor how to properly use it as a javelin. He's supposed to throw it over the ropes as Owens runs up the ramp. Bálor soaks up the knowledge and nods with intent, but after his second throw bounces off the ropes and lands a little too close to where the front row of fans would soon be watching, Levesque has one final piece of wisdom: "Maybe throwing the ladder isn't a good idea after all."

Levesque isn't the type of leader who flies in for tapings, then darts back to Stamford—out of sight, out of mind. He's the true leader of NXT in mind, body, and spirit, taking ownership of the development system unlike anyone before him.

"I was really surprised to see the extent of Triple H's involvement and how hands-on he is behind the scenes of NXT," says Apollo Crews. "For example, my debut was in Brooklyn, and when I was rehearsing my entrance, Triple H came up to me and coached me on how to go about it. In my mind, I was like, 'This is crazy. This is a guy I grew up watching, he's one of the best to ever do this, and he's helping me with my entrance.' He's trying to give me advice that will benefit me—and that blew my mind. You wake up every day, and you're like, 'Is this really my life?' We didn't think it could get any bigger or better than when we went to Brooklyn, but something always comes along that

Triple H shares a moment backstage with Charlotte.

tops it, and then something else tops that. A lot of that is because of how hands-on Triple H is. You can tell that he really loves what he's doing. It's just amazing to have someone around who has been where he's been and has done what he's done."

"I had no idea how WWE worked; I had no idea how NXT was going to work," adds Finn Bálor. "It has been a real learning experience. In Japan, you go out there, and you're left to your own devices. The cameramen are there to catch whatever they can catch. In NXT, you're taught to do moves so that the cameramen can capture the coolest angles and the coolest shots. The attention to detail that goes into producing the show is truly mind-blowing. The amount of time Hunter gives everyone and the knowledge he is willing to share with everyone is mind-blowing. That, for me, is one of the reasons I want to shout, 'This is why I came here!' Getting direction and leadership from someone who has been to the top of this industry is incredible for everyone."

"Triple H has crafted his own brand here in NXT, and the brand is about opportunity," says Terry Taylor. "Triple H gives everybody an opportunity; he has no favorite. If he sees potential in somebody in this system, he will shine a light on that person and let people see them. He encourages them to be themselves and tells them he believes that they can do it. And these women that he has brought up would run through a brick wall for him because they know he would do it for them. These women are talented, athletic, and can do things that half the guys can't do, they have a boss who shows them love, and they have the opportunity to perform with other girls they love and in front of crowds who appreciate them; that's a recipe for success and a blast to watch. The world is always in flux. What's impossible today is possible tomorrow.

"Think about the investment WWE puts into their talent. Everybody here has been vetted with background checks and FBI checks and has had their health checked out. We invest thousands of dollars in people before they even get here. Then our job is to create this persona, this act, this character who will be able to do what they do for an extended period of time. So each talent is an investment in the hopes that in the future, they will make this business better and they will make WWE better."

Making WWE healthier is precisely what Levesque thinks about when it comes to NXT, and a lot of what he does is because he can envision where the business is going with the hindsight of where it already was.

"I learned to wrestle in a warehouse with no heat or air conditioning, and we wrestled inside a boxing ring that had absolutely no give to it," he explains. "If my trainer Killer Kowalski didn't like something you were doing, he didn't politely ask you to do better; he straight up smacked you upside the head with a phone book that was inside a plastic bag so he could swing it at you. If Kowalski could see what I built here, he'd probably tell me I'm making a bunch of pussies. He'd think I'm making them soft—that I'm making it too easy on them—but I'm not making them soft, I'm giving them every tool they need to succeed.

"Every single Superstar who came before them—Hogan, Savage, Warrior, Michaels—all succeeded at the level they did without any of the tools I'm giving today's talent; so the athletes training now have no excuse. If you don't make the cut, it's not because you weren't given the opportunity; it's because you weren't good enough, you didn't have what it takes, or you didn't take advantage of the opportunity. It's as simple as that. I want to give them everything so that there's no excuse for why they didn't make it.

"Nobody has ever had this; something like this has never existed. There has never been this type of video system. There's never been this amount of direct contact between the trainers and the talent. There has never been the connection between the office and the talent. I can watch these guys train from my office in Stamford. Any time I want to see what's happening, 24/7, I can check in and see it live. Any time someone wants to show me something, a character they're working on or a new move, I can see it, and I can give them live feedback. No one has ever had this before. So you can't compare facilities. Talent-wise, now we have athletes from India, Russia, Serbia, Japan, Australia, Canada, Mexico, South America; we're a global brand with a global network and we recruit talent globally. One of our two talents from India came from a small village outside of Delhi and Punjab. He was literally in the middle of nowhere, and we had to go visit his family in a mud hut. He's a national Kushti champion. Kushti is a thousand-year-old wrestling tradition in India, and he's a big deal there. He's a big star and celebrity in India, but there he was living in a mud hut. In the past, he never would've been able to walk out of his mud hut one day and go, 'Hey, I want to be a WWE Superstar. I'm going to move to Stamford.' We found him; we put the feelers out; we talked to him; we cultivated

Bayley gets her arm raised at *NXT Takeover: Respect.*

that relationship. Is he going to make it? I don't know. But in India, it's a huge deal that he's here.

"Look at the talent coming up: Kevin Owens, Charlotte, Sasha, Becky Lynch. If you look at our main roster, 80 percent is either out of NXT or our Performance Center. The Performance Center has been around for only two and a half years, and look at the results. I can look at *WrestleMania 31*, and every single match except mine had talent from the Performance Center and NXT. Seth Rollins, Roman Reigns, Bray Wyatt, and talent after talent after talent. The desire was already there; we're just filling the need. The roster needed new, fresh, young talent, and that's what NXT is delivering, right now and for the future. We're trying to jump out ahead of the curve and get these guys out there for the WWE Universe to see. If we waited any longer to get this started, in a few years we would've been like, 'Oh no, the business is dying. What are we going to do now?'

"We have all this talent on *Raw* and *SmackDown Live*, and guys here are like, 'I'd like to get on the main roster,' but we just don't have an open spot. One, that's a great problem to have, and two, they now work for NXT, the second biggest promotion in the industry, which just happens to be owned by the biggest company in the industry. If you're a top guy on NXT, you're making more money than you were on the indies without having to hustle. No one is saying, 'I had to drive 500 miles and I hope the guy pays me when I get there.' You don't need to print your own shirts or sell your own merchandise. You don't need to budget your gas money or make calls to promoters to find extra work. That's a lot of hassle. NXT? You train every day in a world-class facility. You live in a beautiful area of the country. You're surrounded by motivated people 24/7. And we book you on our shows, which are now, on the smaller side, 500 seats, while our bigger tour is of the 2,000- to 3,000-seat variety. We sold out the Barclays Center . . . that's over 13,000 seats. So if you're a talent out there, would you rather do the hustle on the indies or would you rather be in NXT, sitting in the on-deck circle with your foot in the door? It's like playing AAA for the

Triple H speaks to NXT Superstars on the stage prior to *WrestleMania 32*.

Yankees; you're just waiting for someone to blow out their shoulder so you can get the call up. That's an awesome spot to be in. It doesn't mean they don't want to be called up. It doesn't mean they're not tormented while they're waiting, thinking this is the worst possible situation and wondering, 'Why don't they use me more?' It's a horrifying situation for them, but if they left because they were frustrated about not being called up, they would call me back in a week saying, 'I can't believe I was so stupid. Please bring me back!'

Triple H speaks to Samoa Joe backstage.

"The success has been phenomenal, and that success has led to the NXT brand. We can train these guys to be great in the ring, but they have to learn to be great on television if they truly want to make it. Full Sail is just a micro-version of *Raw* and *SmackDown Live*. One of the best compliments anyone ever gave me came from Summer Rae. She had just started on the main roster, and when I asked how everything was going, she was like, 'The first month was brutal. I didn't get it, and I kept making mistakes. I was so nervous.' But then she was watching them set up the stage before a show in London. She sat there for a long time, and she had this epiphany moment: 'There's the ring, there's the hard camera, there's the jib camera, there's the ramp.' She stopped and thought, 'Oh, it's the *same*.' That night, she went out and was a different performer. It was this eye-opening event. All she had to do on *Raw* is what she had already been doing on NXT. And that's the intent. It's this smaller version of what we do so when you get out there in front

> ## "I want to give them everything so that there's no excuse for why they didn't make it."

of a larger crowd or in a bigger venue, you don't have to think about which way to face or when to look at the camera or how to walk down the ramp or what the hell a jib is. You know where everything is and you know what everything is because you've been doing it for the last two years on NXT. Same with those camera guys and tech guys and sound guys. We've brought these guys up from NXT, and we're morphing them into the product as we move forward. We're all building this future together."

Austin Aries adds, "Triple H is just so invested in NXT and in helping create stars for the next decade or two. Honestly, the only way to do it is to be hands-on. Nobody knows your vision better than you. The best way to realize it is to make sure you're there and that everybody understands what the mission is—and that's exactly how he runs things in NXT."

CHAPTER 15
You Can't Fight Fate

Some started in the indies and some had no training at all before entering the Performance Center, but one thing's for sure: no two stories about how a performer joined NXT are alike.

"I had talked to hip-hop artist Wale, who was a fan of my work and of WWE as well," says Apollo Crews. "He got in contact with Mark Henry, who then got in contact with Canyon Ceman. They sent me an email about going to a tryout in October 2014. I guess you can say the rest is history. It was a pretty rough tryout—probably the toughest thing I've ever done—but it led me to where I am today. It's one of the best opportunities I've ever gotten in my life."

"I was playing football and got hurt," remembers Baron Corbin. "It was just one of those injuries where, for the NFL, I wasn't worth the money risk anymore. So I was checking around and this was something I had wanted to do ever since I was a kid and was going to wrestling shows with my dad in Kansas City. I met this guy named J.D. Hill, who was a music agent, and he knew the music rep for WWE, so he put in a call for me, and WWE reached out to me the next day. Before I knew it, I was on a plane to Florida to spend a week in FCW. They walked me through everything and they wanted to see if this was something I really wanted to pursue, which it definitely was. They gave me a contract after those five days, and I made the move to Tampa, Florida."

"I first started wrestling in a tiny gym in the UK called Hammer-lock Wrestling," says Finn Bálor. "It was just an old 16-foot boxing ring that was converted into a wrestling ring in a bar. So from where I used

Finn Bálor is ready to thrill the NXT Universe in London.

to be . . . it's a wild stretch of the imagination to end up in the Performance Center. Here, we have a state-of-the-art facility and coaches from all around the world. It's a huge difference, but the main thing about any training school is the passion. Regardless of what the facility is like, the one thing you need to have is passion. That's something that the coaches have brought out in all of the performers. They've instilled that passion in us, and we've all risen up as a team, and that's what sets NXT apart. We train together, travel together, and work shows together, and we're all pulling in the same direction as we try to achieve the same dream. There's a real camaraderie in the locker room. We're around each other 24/7, so it's almost like a high school football team. We have a bond and we're invested in each other's personal lives. We're such a tight-knit group, and that brings out the best in everyone in the ring as we try to achieve this greatness together."

Becky Lynch used a match against Paige's mother as a springboard to NXT. "Robbie Brookside is the person I called when I wanted that tryout," Lynch remembers. "And he remembered me. One of my last matches was when I was 19, and he remembers me hitting hard and holding my own against Sweet Saraya, Paige's mother. She has this reputation of being a tough cookie, because she is, so I think that really impressed them. But then I was gone for years, and when I called him he said that he always wondered what had happened to me, so he was excited to have me try out. My tryout was in front of Canyon, William Regal, Robbie Brookside, and Jerry Brisco, and I remember being really star struck by William Regal because I loved watching him when I was younger. He was just the nicest man. I remember being myself at the tryout because I felt like this was what was meant to happen and this was where I was meant to be. I was going to get it."

Being a WWE Superstar is all Sasha Banks ever dreamed of, so when she finally got the opportunity to become a WWE Superstar, she was all-in. "I've loved WWE since I was 10, and once I started watching it, I knew that the only thing that I ever wanted to be was a WWE Superstar. I remember thinking about being in WWE every single waking moment of every single day," she says. "I remember emailing these wrestling schools and asking, 'Can you please train me? How much does it cost to be a wrestler?' And they would always be like, 'You have to be 18, sorry.' When I finally turned 18, I told my mom, 'I'm doing it!' And in Boston at the time, they had this fantasy camp. It was a one-day camp and the person who did the most impressive stuff won three months of free training. I was the only girl, and I remember thinking that this was my opportunity—do or die—and I trained for months beforehand. I was so nervous because I was expecting all these big guys, but I remember walking into that school and seeing a bunch of little teenagers who were fat and out of shape and dressed like Jeff Hardy. So I walked in and I was like, 'Hmm, maybe I do have a chance.' After that day, they chose me and I began my training at the age of 18. I started my journey in the indies in 2010, and I got signed in 2012. Every time WWE came to town, I asked to be an extra and they always said yes. Then I asked for a tryout and they sent me to FCW for a week. I remember I prayed to God; I said, 'God, this is my opportunity—this is my dream—and I'm not gonna leave this place not signed.' So that's what happened, and now I'm here at NXT and I just began on the main roster. I'm living my dream."

Banks, who used to wrestle against her brother while growing up, says her experience training with men has helped her step up her game inside the ring.

"I used to wrestle on my bed and I just felt like I got it. I used to rent movies from Blockbuster about how to be a wrestler and I used to practice with my brother all the time, but when I first began my training, I was so scared because I just didn't want to get knocked out. But then I told myself, 'You've wanted this since you were 10; you cannot be scared. If you get knocked out, good. Then you'll know to not do that again.' It wasn't until five months into my training when I realized I actually wasn't bad at this. There weren't a lot of girls wrestling in my area, and the girls who I did wrestle weren't that great. They were way more experienced than me, and when I would put matches together with them, I knew just by talking to them that I was good at this. I always strived to be the best, and if anybody ever told me I wasn't, I wanted to show them that I was, and that's what I loved so much about training in the indies. I trained with all the guys, and my trainer taught me as an equal. I did everything the guys did. Every time the guys said I couldn't do it, I showed them that I could. I think that's what helped me the most—to be able to prove to people that I can hold my own. I was such a little, scrawny girl—I was 99 pounds when I started—and nobody even wanted to touch me because they were scared that I was gonna break. But I was like, 'No, dude, I'm tough. Let's go right now.' To this day, I'm still one of the smallest, but I'm here to work and show what I have."

Independent hardcore wrestler Drake Wuertz took the NXT tryout hoping to wind up as a performer inside the ring. Eventually, he became an NXT referee. "I was a wrestler on the independent scene for

12 years," says Wuertz. "I wrestled as Drake Younger and I was very fortunate to be able to wrestle in Japan, Mexico, Germany, Scotland, and England. I was able to learn and take my craft all over the world. I had a great run as a wrestler, and I was brought in for a tryout to be on NXT. William Regal pulled me aside and spoke with me about the opportunity to be a referee and how I could contribute positively to this brand. My body had been through a lot—doing the hardcore style for many years—my second child was on the way, and I wanted to do something that made an impact.

"I thought about my longevity and what I'd already done to my body. I had always respected referees so much and appreciated what they'd done, and it was the perfect opportunity to provide for my family, to work in the business that I love so dearly, and to be a part of a brand that was skyrocketing. I just jumped right at it. It was perfect for me. And I really feel that I was meant to be a referee. This is the greatest job in the world. I love being a part of NXT and I love walking into the Performance Center every day and I love being able to help out our young talent here at NXT. It's cool to be able to contribute in that way.

"There's no better feeling than when a talent says, 'Hey, I couldn't have done that out there without you. You were there for me on everything. I really appreciate you.' That is something special. Referees are kind of like ghosts. We're not supposed to be seen until it's time for us to be seen. And it's really special whenever a talent, producer, coach, or even Triple H himself says, 'Hey, you did a good job out there. Thank you.'"

For Enzo Amore, a simple YouTube video led to the realest guy in the room snatching an NXT spot. "I have a different story than most people," he says. "I know people take a lot of different avenues to get here; some people wrestle for 10 years and some people get spotted walking through the mall. I made a YouTube video, and through a mutual friend, that YouTube video was shown to Triple H, who got my phone number and got in contact with me directly. When you're a 25-year-old fan who gets a call from the guy you've looked up to since

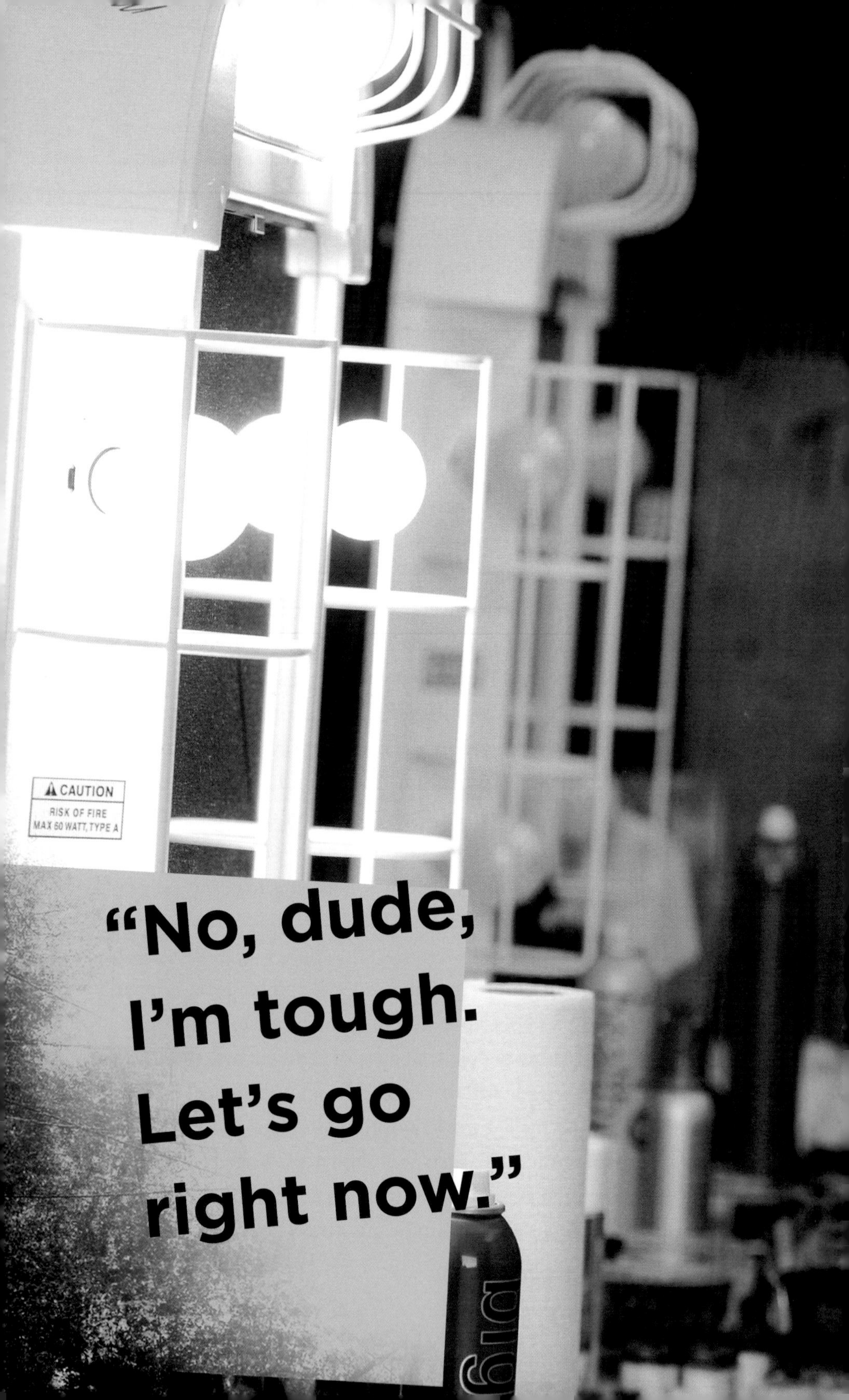

"No, dude, I'm tough. Let's go right now."

Enzo and Big Cass perfected their popular pre-match routine in NXT.

you were a kid, who tells you, 'Hey, we are going to give you a tryout down in Tampa, Florida . . .' Well, I thought it was a prank call; I didn't think it was real life. But I got my tryout with WWE NXT in October 2011, and I was signed in May 2012, so there was some time that elapsed, some fingers that were crossed, and some prayers to the man up top. I was lucky that I had the opportunity to hold a microphone in front of the one and only Dusty Rhodes, The American Dream, at my tryout, and, honestly, if it weren't for him, I wouldn't be here today. So they signed me, and the rest is history.

"When I started out at FCW, it was a dimly lit arena with three rings and, to be fair, about 100 seats," Amore continues. "They did a weekly local episodic TV show. It was good to get on camera and understand your craft as it pertains to working a TV show. But it certainly wasn't going to sell out an arena of 5,000 people like we did in San Jose. When Triple H took over Talent Relations and WWE Development, I think he had a vision. The people walking through the doors of the WWE Performance Center have no idea what it's like to perform your craft in front of 20 people who don't care who you are. There's no global TV show drawing in those audiences; nobody knows who you are. You have to tell them who you are as you come out through the curtain. I had the opportunity to see Sami Zayn work in Madison Square Garden after he debuted on the main roster and the whole crowd was chanting, "OLE, OLE, OLE." It's because they watch NXT. But when Hunter told me I would get to try out in FCW, I thought that was the coolest thing in the world. Holy cow, three rings? A show on local TV? I'm in. Then he tells us, 'Oh, we got this vision for NXT.' Now here we are selling out arenas and people know who we are. You wouldn't have believed it when you heard it come out of his mouth, but it came into fruition."

CHAPTER 16
Hug Life

Watch any live match where there are only a hundred fans sitting on their hands, and it's easy to see that the crowd can make or break you. When it comes to the NXT faithful, their constant chants and rowdy receptions are as much a part of the show as the lights and entrance music. Clearly, Paul Levesque was counting on this when he decided that Full Sail was the place to hold live events. He knew that if he held the tapings at the same place week after week, not only would he be training the talent, ring crew, cameramen, and techs, but he'd also be winning over a loyal set of fans who would make NXT their own.

"I think the WWE Universe looks at us as an alternative," says crowd-favorite Bayley. "They've watched the people on the main roster for a while and maybe they just want something a little different. I feel like there's a lot of relatable people on NXT and a lot of relatable characters who you feel an instant connection with. When NXT started at Full Sail, we had these little shows in Florida that were very intimate. Whether it's a live WWE or NXT show, it's very intimate to be so close to somebody and so close to the ring. I think because we've been in front of them for years and they've been watching us, they kind of respect us, especially since we get to interact with the fans after the shows. They'll wait outside the buildings and we'll talk to them. I actually know a lot of fans by name, so it's a cool relationship. We just got so close to the Full Sail crowd and the Florida scene that it's kind of like they're watching their friends or their kids or they're there to see their kids' idols. There are so many kids who come to our shows, and you get to watch them live their dream, and everybody's so happy for each other. You see the fans Tweet about anybody who debuts at the show, and they're just so happy for them, so it's kind of like a community we've developed. Full Sail has really become a special place, and when the crowd is really into something, you're like, 'Man, this is awesome.'"

One of the most passionate members of the NXT audience is superfan Izzy. The instantly recognizable young girl who's often found sitting in the front row of NXT broadcasts decked out in Bayley's "I am a Hugger" gear and trademark silver headband even became a focal point in the fevered rivalry between Bayley and Sasha Banks. On October 7, 2015, during *NXT TakeOver: Respect*, Banks went into full heel mode, talking trash to Izzy and even stealing her headband to the shock of the Full Sail crowd. Izzy broke down in tears as the fans chanted "Izzy, slap her!"

Bayley embraces superfan Izzy at *NXT Takeover: Respect*.

And while an Izzy slap never took place, Bayley stormed back in to win the match. Izzy's tears of frustration turned to tears of joy when the locker room emptied to celebrate Bayley's incredible victory. Levesque even handed Bayley and Banks flowers to the roar of the crowd, and when Banks finally left the ring, "The Boss" handed her flowers to Izzy as they bumped fists. It is one of the most emotional and memorable nights in NXT history, and it never could've happened if not for the all-in investment the NXT faithful make week after week.

"The NXT fans are diehard," says Becky Lynch. "They will come to every single show, and the support and the love they give is amazing. Since the shows are smaller, there's more of a cult feel to it, and you can feel that energy in the building. But it goes beyond that—our fans follow us from show to show. I did a meet-and-greet at Full Sail for the last TV tapings and there were people from Birmingham—England, not Alabama. There were actually people from Alabama, too, which is amazing. The distance that they will travel is incredible; people will drive six or seven hours for a show in Jacksonville. The fans really support us. Maybe it's because we are smaller and more underground, which makes them feel like they are more a part of it, but it's just unbelievable. And they're incredibly generous; some fans give really personal gifts. With my style being a little bit more steam punk, people have made me these unbelievable cuffs that were decorated with incredible jewels and fine leather, and goggles with all these different cogs and quirks; they are just incredible—unbelievable."

"Everybody watches shows for different reasons," adds Levesque, when asked about what makes the NXT audience unique. "Millions and millions and millions of people watch the Super Bowl. And a lot of them don't really know much about football. They don't watch football every week; they don't have a favorite team—they just cheer for their home team. They're casual fans. It's why it's one of the most-watched things every year. WWE is this massive global entity. You have a lot of different fans who watch the show, and we call it the ultimate variety show. There's a little bit of everything. There's some comedy, drama, there's some soap opera content—there happens to be a lot of things. And it serves those very well. But there's a hardcore group of fans who live, breathe, eat, WWE. Take the NFL, for example. The NFL's not just football, it's the NFL. Anybody can play football; millions of people play football. Only a few have played in the NFL. You could be one of the best football players in the country and not make it to the NFL; same with WWE. We are more than wrestling, we're WWE. Anybody can say they wrestle—anybody, but very few people make it to WWE.

"But NXT has this passionate, driven hardcore fan base too. If you compare it to the NFL, it's the person who knows every stat of every player and every team. They want something different—something a bit more. And that's what we give them. Is it perfect? No. Nothing ever is. But we cater to a different fan base. It's the one thing that I always try to take into account when I'm doing all of this. My goal is to make WWE Superstars, not NXT Superstars, even though I'm doing both. But I want to train them to do all of it; it's not mutually exclusive. With NXT, I'm catering to a slightly different fan base; ninety-nine percent of them watch *Raw* and *SmackDown Live* every single week. But a lot of them probably feel like NXT is more for them because they're so into it, and they drive us. We've created something for them—something that can have a cult following and is a kind of counter-programming to WWE. It's the opposition of WWE, even though it's us. But I think that's part of its charm. I don't want it to be the same; I want it to be different. It's purposely different. It's an alternative. And when I say NXT has become its own brand, that's why. If you're all-in as a fan, then NXT is for you."

And as Levesque taps into the momentum NXT fans are generating on social media, he can see his brand growing across the globe.

"Social media is a global indicator," says Levesque. "One of the hottest spots for NXT is Europe. That's why we set up the European tour. I knew that there was a large following in Japan, too. It was part of the reason that I brought in Hideo Itami in the first place. He's a big star in

Japan, and we have some other stars who came from Japan. I look for talent from all over the world. Like I said before, it doesn't matter what they did or where they come from or how long they've done this. I really don't care. I take what I see and ask myself if I think they can make a great WWE Superstar on any level in any kind of role. And if I do, then I want to have them and try to cultivate them into something more.

"Finn Bálor was a big name in Japan. Neville was a big name in Japan. Hideo Itami was a big name in Japan. I knew there was a following. And I knew the following would translate to NXT and our style. We had an upcoming tour in Japan and I had a plan for NXT to be a big part of that. My original concept was to catch some images of that and plug it back into the NXT show—allow something big to happen internationally and make our brand seem even bigger by piggy-backing on WWE and the fact that those guys are big stars there. That slowly morphed, creative changed, and it got to a point where I was going to have a big NXT Championship Match between Finn Bálor and Kevin Owens in Tokyo, Japan, and I wanted to put it on the WWE live event that was happening there. So I throw out the options: either I loosely shoot this—just to use the footage—or I shoot it, shoot it. So I started to get numbers. What would it cost if I shot only that match, or, just for giggles, what would it cost to shoot the whole show to put on the Network?

"Our contract negotiations were ongoing in Japan, and they were looking for a big hook. I threw it out to our international guys, 'Well, what if we shoot the whole show? The Network doesn't air in Japan, but would our partner in Japan be interested in showing it? Would we be interested in allowing them to have the content if they partnered with us and we took what we wanted for the Network and they took what they wanted for themselves?' Vince was wide open to the idea and the international guys threw it out there, and they jumped all over it. Then we thought, 'Well, let's make it bigger if we're going to put it on the Network. Let's put Brock on there and make it a huge deal.' But at the end of the day, it was still just a non-televised WWE live event that we televised. And the NXT match: Kevin Owens lost the NXT

Championship to Finn Bálor in an epic match, and we tried to make it different with some Japanese culture. I knew the show would be big, I knew our fan base would love the show, and I knew that our Network is comprised of a lot of hardcore fans. But it was the morning of July 4th. When the matches were taking place in Tokyo, Japan, it was 5:30 in the morning in America; 2:30 in the morning if you were on the west coast.

"And it blew up. You put on your badge of honor if you were up at 5:30 in the morning to watch this on the 4th of July. And it became the most-watched program out of all of WWE's pay-per-views on the Network. It was huge. The big indicator for me was when the research came back—with the Network, we can see who watches what, when, and how, and really analyze all of the data—and the most watched thing on that special was Finn Bálor versus Kevin Owens for the NXT Championship. That NXT Championship match was the biggest driving component of a live special with Brock Lesnar and John Cena on it. It was a big card, but they were the most-watched component of it. That was a big moment, not necessarily for me, but for a lot of people in the WWE corporate world; NXT was more than just a development brand. What we were doing was turning into a business. All of a sudden the people inside WWE were like, 'Well, wait a minute. Hold on, the NXT guys did that? And that was the most watched thing on this unbelievably watched product?' I think half of them had thought, 'I don't know if Japan at 5:30 in the morning is a good idea. Who's going to watch it? It's a holiday.' If you build it, they will come."

With NXT fans being so active across social media and so hungry for more action, Becky Lynch isn't surprised by the success of any show—even if it airs pre-dawn.

"The internet has played a major part in building NXT because a lot of the stars have come from underground federations or promotions where they were only seen on the internet," she says. "By getting a lot of people in here who started with this intense popularity on the internet, like Finn Bálor, Kevin Owens, Sami Zayn, and Neville, their

Neville is ready for action.

fan base is drawn to NXT because this is the hub where they all are. So that's been colossal, and it's just a great way to bring everybody in."

When Canyon Ceman looks out at the NXT crowd, he senses something special not only inside the ring, but also in the ringside seats. "I think that the fans love NXT because they sense the passion and commitment of these athletes and the commitment to excellence from Triple H, the employees, the coaches, the trainers, the medical staff," he says. "There is a pride of ownership in this brand that I think is palpable when you watch our show. I also think the female empowerment that's happening is a big part of the allure. When you see the women main-event a live event or a TV taping, that says something that inspires audience loyalty. I also think that these Superstars are telling stories in a smart and interesting way, with a unique and diverse move-set. I don't know if that has ever been true before. Every legend who walks into this building is trying to help them, and they can feel that there is a heritage—that they are standing on the shoulders of giants. I think they can feel that in NXT right now more than any aspiring Superstar ever has before."

"The fans are faithful," adds Kevin Owens. "A lot of them are always at the Full Sail shows, or they follow NXT around Florida, so there are a lot of faces we recognize. I don't know all their names, but you know the fans. It creates a special kind of feeling between the performers and the audience, and I think a lot of them feel like this is as much theirs as it is ours, which is probably why they booed any time we mentioned *Takeover* being in Brooklyn—they wanted it for themselves. But obviously, as this thing gets bigger, we are going to go to different places. *Takeover* being at the sold-out Barclays Center is just so crazy. When I got here in August of 2014 the first show I went to in Tampa had maybe 200 people. It's just wild to see how much it has grown.

"I understand why the fans want to keep it all at Full Sail. To have invested so much—a lot of them have come to every show for the last one or two years—they must feel like this is theirs as well. And it is kind of cool. It reminds me, honestly, of one of the companies I worked for on the independents, called Pro Wrestling Guerrilla. Every show is in the same venue in Reseda, California, and a lot of the fans go every month. The Full Sail audience reminds me a lot of that. So it has been a nice bonus because at the same time I kind of feel like I am back in Reseda, where I did so much and I felt very at home. And I feel very at home here."

And while the NXT audience continues to grow, talents like Bayley continue to appreciate what that growth means to them as performers and use the energy from the crowd to bring more out of their performances. Bayley does something that was passed down from coach Joey

Kevin Owens versus Sami Zayn at *NXT Takeover: Arrival.*

Mercury, who learned it from none other than legendary WWE Hall of Famer Eddie Guerrero. "When they got to shows, when the first match or the opening theme would start, Eddie would peek through the curtain just so he could feel the energy and see what the crowd was like, and he would be able to determine what kind of match he wanted to have from that," says Bayley. "I remember learning that from Joey, who learned it from Eddie Guerrero, and I was like, 'Man, I should do that!' So every show, I peek out during the first match just so I can feel what the people are like that night. When we were at the Barclays Center, I didn't even have to peek out of the curtain to see; I could hear it and I could feel it. I don't even know how to explain it. Walking out is the most nerve-wracking thing ever, but I feel so emotional, like I can't believe this is happening. But once I get in the ring, I think, 'Man, this is amazing.' I could just look up at the bleachers forever, and sometimes I can't even see the people because of all the lights. I could just stand there forever; I'd be happy with just doing my entrance because I get to be with everybody and be happy with them."

Looking out into the crowd is one thing, but it's actually meeting the WWE Universe and talking to them that lights up Bayley's nights. "People from all over the world come up to us and feel like they're the most hardcore fans. It blows my mind. I'm like, 'How do you know who I am?' But we're on their TV, and you hear it from everybody who does tours or signings: fans tell them how much they love NXT. It's still really weird to me, though, whenever we do a show outside of Florida because I still can't believe anybody knows who I am. I remember the first time we went to Columbus, Ohio, and I had a match against Charlotte, and the crowd was so happy to see everybody, but I didn't think they'd know me, so I just went out trying to have fun. But oh my God, the crowd was amazing, and I just thought, 'I'm in Columbus. How do you guys know who I am?' It's the Network; once we got the Network, NXT blew up. More people watch it than we think."

CHAPTER 17
The American Dream

On June 11, 2015, Dusty Rhodes passed away at the age of 69. In charge of promo class, he was the most beloved coach at the Performance Center and helped shape the careers and characters of everyone from Bray Wyatt to Seth Rollins. At the same time, he was known as a father figure to everyone in the building, especially the young development talent who were hundreds, sometimes thousands, of miles away from family.

"People ask me all the time, 'How are you going to replace Dusty?'" says Paul Levesque. "But honestly, you can't. He was more than a coach; he was a presence. Dusty's influence on these kids, on this place, and on everything we do can't be measured."

"When it came to promos, he's the best in the world," says Sasha Banks. "He would sit with me when I would get so frustrated, and he always believed in me, especially when I didn't believe in myself. He would pull me aside and be like, 'Sasha, don't you worry, you're going to be a star.' He never let me give up and he helped me so much."

"I was very fortunate to be able to work with 'The American Dream' Dusty Rhodes for a year before he passed," says Finn Bálor. "I learned a lot from that man. When I first joined NXT, I wasn't the most confident person to ever cut a promo. He told me, 'Finn, before you came here, I didn't know who you were, but by the way people talked about you, I thought Lou Thesz was about to walk through the door. You need to bring your promo skills and your interview skills up to par with your wrestling skills. You have to be the total package if you're

business, but he taught me even more life lessons. And I think that each and every one of those life lessons translates directly to what you see on screen. He taught me to be myself, and he taught me that if you want to be successful in this business, there's only one way to do it, and that's to be real and genuine. I walk through the curtain and I say, 'Bada Boom! Realest guy in the room.' That is all Dusty's doing because Dusty believed in me and what I did while other guys said, 'Enzo, your style on the mic is too fast . . . people can't figure out what you're talking about.' There is a lot of politics that goes on backstage in any business, and this industry is no different. You're going to get a lot of advice from people, and sometimes you're going to get good advice

Triple H and Dusty Rhodes congratulate new NXT Champion Big E Langston.

and sometimes you're going to get bad advice. I never got bad advice from Dusty Rhodes—not once."

Paige is another performer who felt particularly close to Rhodes.

"I was very close to Dusty—extremely close," she says. "He kept me sane when I first came here. He took a shine to me straight away, so he took me in and helped me. He loved to help. He was definitely on the talent's side—he was on our side. He was the voice of reason and our voice when it came to talking to the office. He was always backing us up. Cody Rhodes explained it best: he didn't like the toys that were already packed up and ready to go. He liked the broken toys that he could fix up himself, polish, and then send on their way.

"The American Dream" has a message for the NXT crowd.

"I remember one day in promo class he said to me, 'I don't want you to say very much. You're this mysterious ribbon-haired lady.' So I was like, 'Dusty, I can't just do a promo every week and not say anything. I have to say something, otherwise people are going to get bored of me.' One day I was so frustrated and I gave this really bad promo, and he said, 'I asked you for chicken dinner and you gave me chicken shit.' I was so mad at him, I said, 'You're a motherfucker!' And I flipped him off and walked away. I went up in the women's locker room, and five minutes later, I heard a knock on the door and Dusty said, 'Can I speak to you?' So we sat on the steps of the Performance Center while everyone was still waiting in the promo class, and he said to me, 'I just want what's best for you. I want you to do the best that you can. I know you're going to be a big star someday, and I know you're going to make it. Just listen to me and you'll be on your way.' And then he said, 'You're the first person to ever call me a motherfucker.' I was like, 'Sorry, Dusty, you made me mad.' He was so sweet. He always helped me. He was such an awesome guy."

"Dusty Rhodes has been NXT's greatest teacher," says Charlotte. "It wasn't the promo room that brought all these characters to life; it was Dusty. The promo room is just somewhere to practice. But it does make a huge difference, and it's somewhere you need to go every single day if you want to improve. You need to be able to better your craft, but Dusty was such a huge influence when it came to bringing out these characters."

Another character Dusty helped influence is Bayley. "He used to call me Bayley-Wayley and I'd call him Dreamie-Weemie," she says, laughing. "I remember him Tweeting about me when I first got here. He wrote, 'Bayley's really good in the ring.' He didn't tag me or anything; I just happened to see it and I freaked out. I used to go to him all the time and say, 'What do you need me to do? How do I better myself?' Even when I had a character started up, I always felt like I needed more and more, and he would give me little ideas. And I would do it and he would love it, and next thing you know, I'd be doing it

"The American Dream" Dusty Rhodes, 1945–2015.

on TV. Actually, he was the one who helped me with the ponytail. I came out with a ponytail for my first match as Bayley, and before the match I took it out because I didn't think that it would be okay to have a ponytail. When I came backstage, he said, 'Never take your hair out again. Leave it up in the ponytail.' And now it's a signature thing, so I can thank him for that as well. He was amazing."

Canyon Ceman adds, "I love to talk about Dusty. Getting to know him over the last three years has been a great honor. I mean, the man's a legend. There was the on-screen character Dusty, and there was the guy whose office you'd walk into and who you couldn't stop talking to because you were so entertained and amused. And sometimes it was like, 'Oh my God, did you just say that?' But Dusty's influence on the Performance Center and on the NXT development system will never go away. I consider him the heart and soul of this building. The day the news came of his passing was a really, really hard day here. Everybody was in shock, and it's because he touched everyone so deeply—not because he made them a better performer, but because he was a beautiful human. He was just an amazing person who made you feel great when you were in his presence. He was obviously funny, obviously charismatic, but he also cared about you. He was the kind of guy who left you a positive message when he really didn't need to. The kind of guy who texted you when he heard something that meant he might need to check in on you. He cared about you as a person. I told my parents and my wife when Dusty Rhodes called me 'Boss.' It was the day before he died, and that's a unique privilege in my life. To have earned his respect and enjoyed his amazing personality was one of the best parts of this job. Dusty loved this group of people—the coaches and the talent— and he wanted them to become better performers, but he also helped them become better people. And they will all, myself included, look back on him as influential, not just in their careers, but in their lives."

CHAPTER 18
Data and Mirrors

While the first floor of the Performance Center is all business, with its seven rings and weight room, the second floor is no less important. In fact, the mirror room is where characters come to life, or go to die. Adjacent to the WWE Founding Father's Wall, where pictures of legends like Andre the Giant and Bruno Sammartino inspire young performers,

the room is set up so that a performer can walk in at any time of day, cut a promo in front of a camera, and then watch it back immediately on an iPad. Back in the day, Superstars would cut promos in front of mirrors in the locker room or in their car in order to practice before a big show, hence the old-school name for new-school technology. Once the promo has been cut and saved under their ID, performers are then able to ask for instant feedback from peers and coaches or delete the entire thing and start over if they come to the realization that it belongs on the editing room floor rather than in the spotlight of NXT.

This is the room where the careers of Bray Wyatt and Tyler Breeze were revitalized, thanks to the countless hours they spent perfecting their craft. It's also the room where talent practice their mic work before introducing the character to their peers in the more-official promo class, which separates performers into groups (women, big guys, teams, characters, smaller guys, foreign accents) to work on their speaking skills in front of a critical but honest audience of coaches and fellow development talent.

"For us, promo class and the mirror room is where we can try things that we may not be able to try on TV," says Crews. "You might have an idea of something you want to do, and it might sound good in front of your mirror at home, but when you get to promo class and cut it in front of your peers and coach, you'll get an honest opinion. I might cut a promo in my house and think it's the best thing in the world, but when I do it in front of them, it's just mediocre. The mirror room enables you to try different things in front of a camera, then watch it back and see how it sounds. The most difficult thing is performing in front of your peers, but it's so important to get that honest feedback. Since you're trying to impress them, it's a great way to come out of your shell and think outside the box. For us as performers, being able to communicate is very important. Cutting a promo is one of the keys to success in this business, so having the tools and being able to go into that mirror room as often as we want is so vital. You're able to see your strengths, your weaknesses, and whether or not you need

Tyler Breeze inside the mirror room.

NXT Superstars get instant feedback from peers in the green-screen room.

to approach your promo with different energy or different emotions. Not everybody is The Rock. Not everybody has those tools early on in their career. When I was wrestling in the indies, I didn't cut a lot of promos. I didn't get the chance to talk a lot, so one of my main focuses is getting better at cutting promos. I'm really working hard to improve my communication skills.

"It's so important to have the technology to watch your promos and your matches. When you're in the middle of it, you think it comes off a certain way, but when you watch it back, you see exactly what you need to fix. Before the Performance Center, I rarely had the opportunity to do that, and even if I did have the opportunity to watch a match back, I couldn't ask for feedback from someone who has years of coaching and performance experience, like we're able to do at the Performance Center. We have all the tools for success here. If someone fails, it's because they're not taking advantage of all the opportunities they are being given."

"I hated being in front of a camera. I didn't have a character," says Bayley, "and I had no idea what to talk about aside from how much I love WWE, and, really, everybody here loves WWE. Then I came here and Dusty Rhodes forced me to do promos. He would make me do them over and over again, and there were so many times when I'd end up in tears. I'd say, 'I just don't want to do this.' I'd question whether I really wanted to be here; I just hated being in front of the camera. We'd have special classes with the people who needed the most work and, of course, I was always one of them. Dusty Rhodes pushed you and pushed you to be the best performer you could be.

"It's embarrassing to watch, or even think about, my old stuff. There are some writers here who used to come to our promo classes and they'll say, 'Remember when I made you cry?' I guess that's what helped me. I needed that push and that tough love. Dream was amazing for that because he also inspired you and he believed in you."

Now, Bayley sees her promo skills as one of the things that connects her to her fans. "I think they can feel the passion that I have and that I'm really just this little kid inside who's so happy to be here. But I know I need to focus on the business, too. I need to fulfill my dreams. I have to learn how to tone down my stuff and talk to people and connect with them without breaking down and crying because I'm nervous. I just tell myself everything's okay—that's what Dream always told me: 'Everything will be okay. Just tell your story.' Dream was really good; he was the best character and promo teacher ever. Now, Ryan Katz (creative producer behind the scenes at NXT) is taking over, and he's doing a great job and giving us new challenges."

Sasha Banks is another performer who stepped into promo class without a word to say but has since worked to juice up her character. Now, she's one of the best in the business.

"I was so nervous," admits Banks. "I would freeze anytime I saw that red light go on. I think because I didn't have a character, I didn't know what to talk about. All I knew was that I love wrestling, but you need to have more than that. You have to have this big personality and

Sasha Banks puts the finishing touches on her "Boss" persona.

persona, and it wasn't until I finally found the Boss character that it clicked. Because that's what I truly felt inside: that I was the best. Maybe I'm a little cocky, but I had to turn it up because I always got walked on. I had to wait for my opportunity and I was always very patient because there were girls who were getting their opportunities. And I would just sit there and I would wait and wait and wait. I would get so frustrated that they wouldn't use me, and I remember just sitting in that auditorium at Full Sail and watching their matches, thinking,

A look inside the promo room.

'What am I doing wrong? Why am I not on TV? How can I get myself there?' And I really thought about what I was missing. And I realized I was missing a character. So I came up with the Boss. Now, put me in front of a camera and I'll talk for days."

"With promos, the key is practicing, so you can find your voice and gain confidence," says Neville. "From the moment you walk into the building to the moment you leave at night, that mirror room is open for you to practice your promos and watch them back immediately to review your look and sound. The promo room is a huge part of the Performance Center."

But Charlotte admits, "I can't watch myself; I hate watching myself. But I do find that the best promos are the ones you can personally relate to somehow. It's not necessarily how *you* feel, but if you can relate what you're saying to something you feel inside—those promos are usually the best."

When it comes to watching their own performances, it's not all about the promos. Every student inside the Performance Center has the ability to watch anything, from taped practices to matches to any pay-per-view in WWE history (when they want to study the legends). Next to the mirror room is a lounge where talent eat breakfast and lunch and huddle around giant screens that showcase the best talent in the world.

"It's one thing to come back from a match and have someone tell you something, but it's another thing to step into a film session and watch your match while a trainer explains what happened and shows you areas to improve," says Big Cass. "When you watch it as an outsider, you can see what they're talking about. Watching your matches is so important because you can get multiple coaches' opinions at the same time. You can see what they're talking about. You can learn things about yourself that you like or don't like. It's pretty cool."

Cass also enjoys sitting in the film room and working on his announcing skills.

"You sit in the room with the TV, and you take on the role of announcer," says Cass. "I've done it a couple of times. It's great when you're in there with someone like Byron Saxton, who knows what he's doing. He'll guide you along and spoon-feed you some stuff. Calling matches is so difficult. Until you're in that room with your headset on and have completely run out of things to say, you just don't realize how difficult announcing is. It's a great thing about the Performance Center; they want you to learn all aspects of the business, not just what you're doing inside the ring."

CHAPTER 19
The Call-up

The Performance Center might be the premiere training facility in the industry, but that doesn't mean the graduation process is straightforward. It's not like you finish Terry Taylor's class and walk down the ramp on *Raw* the next night. In fact, while Paul Levesque has 100 percent say over everything that happens inside of the Performance Center and NXT, the one aspect he has no control over is who Vince McMahon actually calls up to the main roster.

"Vince makes the final decision on who gets called up," says Levesque. "I make suggestions and show him who I think is ready and who is not, but it's totally his call. Sometimes, I say, 'Vince, this person is ready,' but Vince will say, 'I just don't see it.' So I need to convince him that this person will make it on the main roster. Other times, Vince will say, 'Hey, I've heard a lot of buzz about this guy. Let me see him.' And I show him a tape, and he's called up. Bray Wyatt is a guy like that. I showed Vince a rough vignette package, a video we shot to show him who the character is, and he loved it so much, he wanted to put it on *Raw* that Monday. We didn't even edit the vignettes that we shot down here; that's what ended up on *Raw*. Other times, Vince will say, 'Got any big guys down there? I have this idea for a really big guy.' So it really just depends on the need; it depends on what he wants and on what he's looking for that day. Who gets called up is his decision.

"Who boils up—who gets the spotlight down here—is my call. He doesn't touch anything that happens down here. And he has said, 'I don't want to touch it because I'll screw it up.' He has a different vi-

Triple H gives instruction prior to an NXT event.

sion than me, but what makes it work is that different vision. Neither vision is wrong; it's chocolate and vanilla. Vince likes chocolate, and I like vanilla. WWE and NXT are completely different products, and that's a good thing. He'll ask me, 'What women would you bring up? How would you do it?' So I'll give him suggestions, but at the end of the day, what happens on *Raw* and *SmackDown Live* are his decisions. Those calls are all his. I make suggestions—we all make suggestions—but it's his choice. Everything down here is up to me. NXT talent, creation, storylines, that's my call. Except when I'm smack dab in the middle of a storyline and he says, 'Oh, by the way, I'm taking three of your female Superstars.' I'm thrilled, and I want them to be successful, but sometimes you have to get really creative when writing the show. People are looking at the women and say they created the Revolution, but Charlotte, Sasha, and Becky left; so then it was up to Bayley to carry the torch and for us to find new women to keep the momentum

moving forward. That's just how the call-up process works. It forces us to constantly build new Superstars because we just don't know who will still be with us in the next few months."

At the same time, having no control over call-ups has also worked in Levesque's favor. When people get frustrated with not getting brought up to the main show, they know not to blame their boss.

Former WWE and NXT champ Seth Rollins says that while the development system has changed, it's still the performer's passion that matters most when it comes to whether or not someone gets the call to the main roster. "If you have the right frame of mind heading into the Performance Center, you will be successful," says Rollins. "But if you come from a background where you've never really had to struggle in your life and you've had things handed to you, you're going to fall apart pretty quick. First of all, the amount of work that they put in there is pretty incredible. Between the talent, the coaches, and the entire staff, it's a living, breathing life form. It's NXT 24 hours a day, seven days a week. I came from a different place. I paid to train in a shipping warehouse in Chicago in the winter. To go from that to sunny Orlando, Florida, and being paid to learn how to become a Superstar in a sterilized environment—there are pros and cons to it. If you come in and you're already jaded and you've already kind of been given certain allowances, you're going to fall off because your work ethic won't be there. You have to come in with the right state of mind. I never trained in the Performance Center. I trained in the warehouse when it was still FCW, and every day was a grind. And even then, I probably took it for granted sometimes. But comparing the two, FCW was a dingy little warehouse. It wasn't spectacular. We didn't have this cult following. We didn't have people waiting outside, trying to get our autographs. We didn't have a show on the Network or anything like that. So I think, to an extent, it's about the person rather than the environment. If you let yourself get swept away in the magic of the Performance Center, you're going to fail because you'll lose your passion, and passion is the number one factor for success in this industry.

If you have passion, you can be successful no matter where you train or what environment you work in.

"It can be a very difficult process. The waiting period for me was two years down in FCW. It was an island off on its own, but I really enjoyed the time I spent there: building relationships with the other guys, traveling the back roads of Florida, doing shows in little towns. And at the end of the day, I was being paid to train. It was a steady job. I got to wrestle and go to sleep in my own bed every night. Overall, it was a very good experience for me. I really enjoyed the process, but there was a ton of frustration that went along with it. Hindsight is 20/20, and, sure, it's a lot easier to be happy about it now than it was back then. If I could go back in time, I'd tell myself to take it a little easier.

"It doesn't really matter what environment you're in; what matters is what you bring to the table as an individual," continues Rollins. "I've seen people from all walks of life train in a ton of different environments. And I've seen them be frustrated for years or get bumped up in months. The success rate is variable. There's no right way or wrong way to do it. It all depends on whether the individual wants it bad enough and has the passion, the love, and the desire for what we do. I knew I was working harder than everybody else. I knew I was putting in the time and I knew what I could bring to the table. It was just a matter of patience. And it was a battle of attrition. I just had to wait it out and not give up."

"People always think they should be called up earlier, and they get impatient, but these kids need to learn how to stay the course," says Terry Taylor. "People watch WWE on TV and think they can do it, but if we send them up too soon, they'll fail. It's not easy. It's hard and it's demanding. John Cena has spent 13 years on top—it's unheard of and unbelievable to have a run like that, but these kids think they can do it. You don't know what you don't know until you get up there. We just want to make sure they're as ready and as prepared as possible, so that when they leave here, there's less of a transition. Every college football player thinks he can play in the NFL until he gets to training

Paige becomes the first-ever NXT Women's Champion.

camp. And then it's like, 'Oh my God, I was the fastest in college, now I'm the fifth fastest on this team. These guys can do everything better than me.' These kids have to figure out the same thing. They might leave here as the best in NXT, but when they get to *Raw*, they still have a lot to learn."

And while Levesque isn't making the call on who joins the main roster, he has plenty of advice for the NXT talent looking to become WWE Superstars.

"Sometimes, there's an X-factor that you can't put your finger on," says Levesque. "Some talents are magnificent on paper, but they never amount to anything. This guy's got every tool conceivable, but it just doesn't click—nobody cares. And then sometimes a guy on paper makes you say, 'I don't get it.' Kevin Owens, for example, was a guy who I was aware of for a long time, but it took me a little while to really get it. I would see bits and pieces of him here and there, but I wasn't sure. And that's not a knock on him, it's just a fact. But I kept looking because I was interested—otherwise I would've written him off a long time ago—and slowly but surely my interest started to grow. I wanted to see more. I started to watch more. And then I started to go, 'Okay, this kid's got the X-factor.' You can't put your finger on why it works; there's just something there. There's a charisma there—an innate confidence, an innate comfort, an innate whatever it is. It doesn't look like he'd be a great athlete, but he is. And at the end of the day, I'm very interested in his promos. But he's not like Bray Wyatt or The Rock or somebody who impresses you the first time you hear one of his or her promos. He's one of those guys who leaves you thinking, 'I'm not sure why it was great, but he said some really great stuff there.' And he just kind of stays with you; he's honest and simple, and yet it all works. And when you tie all the pieces together, it's an impressive overall package. He has Superstar written all over him. He was one of the guys I went to Vince about, and I said, 'I want you to see Owens. And you're not going to be interested at first. Sit on it. Watch it a few times. And it'll grow.' It was the same thing with Paige. When I first suggested bringing up Paige, he wasn't enamored. A month or two later, we were sitting in gorilla [the stage area behind the curtain] and he looked at me and said, 'I know exactly what you're talking about now. It took me a couple of months, but, man, she's good.'

"Sometimes, it takes a while to connect all the pieces. Every now and then, you'll find a guy who has a bunch of pieces that don't connect, but and when you watch them work all together, you find yourself realizing, 'Wow, they're just really, really good.'"

For call-ups Becky and Sasha Banks, their promotion was both exhilarating and bittersweet. "For months, I had heard rumors and rumblings that the Four Horsewomen would be brought up, but nothing

> **"I just had to wait it out and not give up."**

happened," says Banks. "And every week, I would watch *Raw* and they would talk about change, change, change. But I didn't hear anything from the office, so I finally gave up because I thought, 'I'm not going to stress when I have something so good here at NXT.' Then I got the call from Mark Carrano (WWE's vice president of Talent Relations) on a Friday or Saturday, and he said, 'This may be it. It may not be. But we're going to bring you to TV.' I've been here almost three years, and I've learned that you can't get too excited over stuff until it actually happens—so I was just like, 'Okay, I'm not going to think that this is my debut because things can still change.' But deep down inside, I was terrified. I was scared for change because we have it so good here in NXT, and the women in NXT are unbelievable; I didn't want to give that up for what I saw on *Raw*. I remember the day I walked into the arena and we got pulled into the office—Becky, Charlotte, and I— and Carrano said, 'We're still waiting for the final call from Vince, but there's a 50/50 chance that you're going to debut tonight.' Again, I was like, 'Don't believe it until it actually happens.' I remember standing in gorilla in my gear and I could hear the fans and my heart was trembling and I was shaking. And then I heard Stephanie McMahon introduce me and my music hit, and it happened. That feeling is indescribable. I was

Becky Lynch debuts as part of the Divas Revolution, on July 13, 2015.

so in the moment that when I walked out, I thought I heard crickets—I thought I heard no reactions—I was just like, 'Ah, whatever! Just do you!' But I watched it back and it was so loud, I was just so nervous and scared. I remember being in that ring and that moment when Nikki bumped into me. I was just like, 'Oh, hell naw,' and I bumped her back. It was just so cool. You always dream of your debut, and I was so terrified that the moment was going to be a mess. But when it happened, it just felt so right. After I walked back through the curtain, I thought of everything I had ever been through and I just burst into tears. My heart felt so full of joy. I was twenty-frickin-three and I had just made my main roster debut. It was insane."

"It's bittersweet. I am gaining a whole new fan base because *Raw* and *SmackDown Live* are seen by so many people," Becky Lynch says. "And I am gaining this massive opportunity to perform on a bigger stage. I want to make women the main-event attraction for *Raw* and *SmackDown Live* and to be seen as the biggest stars this industry has ever had. I want our division to be the thing that people can't miss. And I feel like I'm getting the opportunity to reach as many people as possible and change the entire world's perception of how women are viewed, especially in this industry. I take that as a serious challenge and a really serious mission. But on the flip side, NXT has become this incredible entity and it's the most supportive environment, with incredible coaches and incredible talent, and it's just getting bigger and better. It's going to take over the world. I hope I'll always be a part of it. The Performance Center is somewhere that I'll always come back to and I'll keep training here, but I miss being here every day. I used to love coming in here and seeing all my friends and getting to train and lift weights and do promos. It's a wonderful million-dollar facility that I won't get to come back to as much, but it's always going to be here whenever I want to return."

For Head Coach Matt Bloom, seeing his students graduate to the main roster is one of the most gratifying experiences of his professional career.

"I love it," Bloom says. "Neville and I grew to have a nice little friendship. To see him go up there and do so well—I love it. To see these ladies that are going up there right now—Sasha Banks and Becky and Charlotte—it's incredible to know that we were part of that and helped mold them into WWE Superstars. Every one of those four I just named came to NXT with one dream: make it to WWE. And they've done it and I had a little part in making that dream come true. And that is gratifying beyond words."

CHAPTER 20
Don't Just Get Hyped, Stay Hyped

Paul Levesque sees NXT's success as a reflection of his ability to change with the times and implement refreshing, new ways to develop talent. "You can't just throw somebody out in the woods and say, 'Fend for yourself,'" he explains. "There's the old adage, the bird pushes the baby out of the nest, and he either flies or drops to the ground and dies. That's life, right? Or maybe you slowly teach them how to fly, and eventually they take off on their own.

"I think there's a difference in how people learn today. People can get too comfortable at the Performance Center, so I like to tease them now and then by sending them on the road to *Raw* and *SmackDown Live*. If they think what they're doing here is awesome, when they get there, they say, 'Oh my God, I want that.' You have to keep them hungry because that hunger leads to progress. The hardest part is when they're ready, and they have to wait for a spot to open up. Sometimes, being in development is like purgatory. You're ready and you're just sitting and waiting and it seems like forever; it's the hardest part. I've had the same conversation with Seth Rollins, Dean Ambrose, and Bray Wyatt, and I've told them all the exact same thing: 'Trust me. When it happens, you'll forget about all this. It seems like forever and like it'll never end. It seems like the worst scenario imaginable for you. But one day you're going to get that call and you're going to forget about all of it.' That's what you have to keep in front of them.

Sasha Banks traps Charlotte in a leg lock.

"But to do that, you need to find people who are self-motivated. If you're just going to wait for the crowd to pick you up, then you're in the wrong place. You have to be willing to go out in front of 2,000 people in Peoria who are indifferent toward you. You got to go out there and make them stand up and go crazy. You have to make them leave that building and say, 'Oh my God, that was the greatest show I've ever seen. I'm coming back.' You can't think, 'Well, they paid their money, there aren't many of them, and they're not very excited, so I'm just going to go through the basics and leave.' That's not how you build a business. You have to prove yourself every day. You have to give people more than their money's worth every day, so they want to come back and they want to tell their friends to go see this show. You can never take success for granted. You want those motivated people, and you find out who they are by letting them do this every day. Sometimes, it's like Groundhog Day here; they're running the same drills and it seems like they're doing the same thing every day. They're learning, but they don't even know they're learning. You see who doesn't thrive in that environment. You see who doesn't motivate themselves to grow more. I don't want to have to tell them, 'Go practice your promos.' I don't want to have to tell them, 'Go work on this or that.' The ones who are motivated will do it because they want to be better. Those people will succeed here. The others will fall by the wayside. Does it bother me that I have to spend a bunch of money on people who don't want this bad enough? Yeah, but I'll gladly spend the money on the people who do."

And as NXT continues to grow, Levesque becomes even more proud of the talent Stephanie McMahon refers to as "his kids."

"Obviously I'm proud of my career in WWE and the things that I did and the things I've accomplished," says Levesque. "But I think I get just as much satisfaction and enjoyment out of watching these men and women succeed in NXT. Creating this environment, creating this show . . . it's almost more rewarding and more fulfilling. Steph has told me she loves watching me when my guys are out there. Dusty used to call them his NXT kids, and none of NXT's success could've taken place without him. As much as I did, Dusty was always an assurance by my side. I would just look at Dusty, and he'd give me the 'I agree with you' nod. And I would know he was thinking, 'I'm not going to say it in front of everybody, but I agree with you and we're going the right way on this.' Because sometimes everybody in the room disagrees with you, but you still have to go in the way you feel is right.

"And now, we're seeing the work from NXT pay off on the main roster, like when Seth won the WWE Championship or the Divas Revolution took over *Raw*. I was sitting at the edge of my seat watching them do their stuff on NXT, and now I get to watch on the next level. I'm involved in every component of what they do, and I'm so excited when its good and I'm so happy for them and so proud of them. It's like saying, 'I'm proud of my career, but watching my kids succeed is more fulfilling to me than anything I did.' And I feel that way even

though there are a lot of people responsible for their rise.

"Being involved in their success and watching them reach their potential is just so fulfilling. You are a small piece in helping them get there; taking pride in how good they've become and what they do with it is awesome. It's like being a parent and watching your kid compete and bursting with pride at their success."

Cesaro also takes pride in NXT's success, but the brand's rise doesn't surprise him.

"I'm not surprised by its growth, and it's not quite as fast as people think," says Cesaro. "NXT has actually been going on for a few years. It started very hot, and it's still very hot, and when you combine that with the great production value and the WWE Network, you're able to sustain that momentum.

"NXT is what the future holds, and that is very good for the future of the industry. NXT has a very young audience. Back in the day, they used to refer to them as internet fans, but now everyone is an internet fan. If you want to know anything about a football player, you Google him. If you want to know anything about a WWE Superstar or someone who is signed to NXT or someone who just received a development deal, you Google them, and then you go to YouTube and find videos of matches and interviews and whatever you're looking for. Even young people these days are very knowledgeable because they just go on the internet and read everything they can. There is such a wealth of knowledge for people, and even though NXT has such diverse Superstars, you have all the tools to learn about them. The WWE Universe is so passionate that *Raw* and *SmackDown Live* may not be enough for them. They want to learn more and see more, and now you have NXT to fill that void. It's just this different, raw atmosphere that sucks you in if you love wrestling."

And it's that love of wrestling and that passion for the ring that helped Sami Zayn introduce NXT to the masses. "I wanted to be a part of WWE, period," he says. "I worked long and hard on the independents and I did everything I set out to do—for the most part. I had a really fulfilling career, but this is really the only place I wanted to end up. I didn't want to start here. I really looked up to guys who took the journey around the world before ending up here, and that's who I modeled myself after. Things really went according to plan, so I can't complain. But when I first got here, NXT wasn't a thing. It was a show, but it wasn't a thing. I want to work for companies that have a buzz and are relevant; if this wasn't relevant, my goal was to make NXT relevant. I do think I helped with that. I don't think I was the sole reason, by any means. A lot of people had the same mindset going in. We didn't want to be obscure. We wanted to be a part of something that was being talked about. We wanted to be a part of something that was hot. I think that's a lot of what went into making NXT so hot, and

Becky Lynch with a leg drop on Bayley at *NXT Takeover: Rival*.

now, look at what it has become. I don't know if I'm giving myself credit here, but I definitely feel like one of the forefathers in the early revolution of NXT, alongside Cesaro, Neville, Bo Dallas, and Tyler Breeze. These were the guys who were on the ground floor, chugging away to earn the reputation that NXT now has. I look at NXT with a lot of pride, like in a weird parental role. I know I'm not the father of NXT, but in a weird way, I almost feel like I am a parent.

"We never really spoke to Paul about his early premise for the brand, but once it started rolling along and picked up steam, we really started to see his vision, and he started to vocalize where he wanted to go. Of course, you want to please your boss and everything, but at the end of the day, we believed what we were doing was important, so it became important. I think that's the synergy that needs to exist in order for something to catch on. If the people who are doing it believe it's important, then the WWE Universe will believe it's important, and they will give you their passion. And that's what happened with NXT."

Ultimately, as that passion for NXT grew, so did that fan base. "I think NXT is going to keep growing, but in a weird way, I have this fear that it's going to be like a favorite band you see in a local club," explains Corey Graves. "When you see them in that club, they're the coolest band ever and you love them. But when they get more popular and you have to go to an arena to see them, it's just not the same. I think if NXT keeps growing, it's going to lose some of its intimacy. In a weird way, that's a good thing. This third brand is developmental, and it was never supposed to be anything more than a place to learn. It has grown into a full-blown brand that's now almost in direct competition with our main brands. It's a good problem to have."

To Canyon Ceman, NXT's success isn't just about its popularity or the graduation of its talent. How the talent does once they appear on the main roster is another source of pride. "What excites me the most about the talent who have graduated to the main roster is not so much that they made it, but how they are doing there," says Ceman. "They're launching and making bold impressions with their in-ring skills and

their ability to execute under pressure. And that is a direct reflection of this talent development system, and I am very proud of that. The most recent examples are Kevin Owens, Neville, Charlotte, Becky Lynch, and Sasha Banks. From the moment they make their debut, they are right at the top of the card, and their matches are killing it. And those men and women have launched themselves to where everyone wants to be.

"Once they leave, however, the question remains: how do we keep it fresh? The single coolest part of this job and this industry is that there are no two days that are the same. It's constantly evolving, and that's a reflection of Vince McMahon. He's a visionary, and just when you think you've reached the goal, he changes where the end zone is. In a way, you're like, 'Oh God, I thought we were already there.' But then you go, 'Oh my God, that's great, now we have this new goal to seek.' A great example of this is China. A while ago, China was not really a thought, even though it's a big market. Then I got a directive to find Chinese talent. So every day there is a new challenge that we are asked to fulfill. And now we have two new reality shows that are coming out of this building. We have 16 new talent, six of whom don't speak English as a first language, so how do we make them better performers? First, you have to communicate with them. How do you communicate with a man from North India? Every day, there's an opportunity to learn something. I get to learn all these new sports that I didn't really understand the culture of. The coaches here have to find a way to communicate to a person who is a national Kushti champion of a country of 1.3 billion people, and they have to take him from the bottom of this new industry that he just joined and make him a new star. Every individual is a challenge. How do we take this raw piece of clay and mold it into something that the WWE Universe will love, or hate? It's great."

When Enzo Amore looks back at NXT's early success, he recognizes that the team effort was aided by the creation of the Performance Center itself. "I think NXT has become the brand it is because of the Performance Center. I don't think you can point to the Performance Center alone, because there was a lot of work done before, but I think

NXT the Future Is Now

> **"It's like being a parent and watching your kid compete and bursting with pride at their success."**

that the same people who walked through these doors were the same people putting in the work. The world is at your fingertips at the Performance Center. It is literally your fault if you fail; you can't blame anyone other than yourself. When they put the world at your fingertips, they literally put the ball in your court, and you decide what to do with it. The growth of that brand is directly attributed to Triple H, and his vision for what NXT could become and his belief in the people who are a part of it. We're given freedom as performers—whether it's me on a microphone or the artistry you see in an NXT ring—and some of the greatest matches have taken place right down here at NXT. What we've started has grown to a level on a global scale. At *WrestleMania* weekend in San Jose, 5,200 people bought a ticket to see NXT. We sold out an arena, and people were outside scalping tickets. You couldn't get a ticket. And we have become one of the hottest shows in Orlando, where you have a lot of amusement parks. And I meet fans at Full Sail from all over who say they booked their vacation around attending a NXT taping. So we owe it to the fans, who make that atmosphere so live. Those fans make that show so special, and the people who are watching at home see the hype behind some of the characters on their TV. All of a sudden, the fans at Full Sail started saying my introduction with me: "S-A-W-F-T. SAWFT!" And apparently, in San Jose, those people had been saying it to themselves in their home because they knew all the words to it too, and it has to do with the brand.

"NXT is a brand, it's not developmental, and the Performance Center door is open for business. So when you get signed to a WWE developmental contract, you're really signing a business contract and it's time to go to work. That work translates on a television screen. The belief that the training staff has in us starts with our head coach Matt Bloom, but it really trickles down from Triple H. I had the opportunity to train with Billy Gunn. Some of these coaches are guys who we watched as kids, and they've given us the tools—whether it be in front of green screens, in a weight room, or inside the state-of-the-art facilities—to instill confidence in us in the ring and on a microphone. When you watch NXT live, you are watching countless hours of work come to fruition.

"I think the charm of NXT directly correlates to the amount of work that people put in behind the scenes. Perhaps the average viewer isn't aware, but I think a lot of fans out there know that we come to work on Monday, and we do shows on Thursday, Friday, Saturday, and sometimes on Sunday. Some days are longer than others, and there are weeks when we have no day off. The WWE Universe appreciates that people are putting in hours and are in the ring from nine to five. When you watch NXT, you see a bunch of people who are hungry, who earned that TV time, and who want to make the most of it. And I think most of us, if not all of us, do."

In Amore's opinion, the NXT work ethic is not only contagious, but it has also helped build camaraderie among the roster, leading to even more success as the team works together to help build NXT's future.

"When you see a fellow NXT Superstar debut, whether it's on a pay-per-view or *Monday Night Raw*, there's a sense of pride knowing that you trained with that guy, that you got behind the wheel and drove three or four or five hours to perform in front of audiences on a much lesser scale," says Amore. "At times, we are doing shows in front of 200

Baron Corbin displays his punishing offensive style.

people; at other times, we are doing shows in front of 5,000 people—
but, either way, it's an audience. That's what we want here at NXT. We
put the work in during the week, so when the weekend comes and we
get the chance to perform in front of live audiences, we let it all hang
out. We work together so that the blood, sweat, and tears that you put in
front of a live audience means something. When the same guy that you
wrestled Saturday night goes out there on *Monday Night Raw*, and he's
suddenly a household name and you hear the audience start chanting
'NXT! NXT!' you know that it's not all for nothing. It lets you know that
there is a light at the end of the tunnel because, ultimately, everyone in
NXT wants to be on the main roster. But a lot of us aren't in a rush to
go anywhere; we are part of something special here. This NXT brand
is creating its own buzz. There's a lot of wrestling around the world
that a lot of people don't know is going on because of WWE. This is
sports-entertainment, and this is the Mecca for sports-entertainment,

but some would say the second biggest brand in the industry is NXT."

As he watches his baby grow, Paul Levesque looks for the right balance between business and development. Because of this, he sees the long-term value of treating NXT as the world's most popular wrestling school as more important than the quick buck they might make by bringing NXT to cable television. Part of what has made NXT so special is the fact that it is not overexposed. Once the brand is on cable TV, you then have outside influences pushing for angles that might not be in the best interest of the brand.

"I honestly think if we put it out there, networks would want it," Levesque says. "But the question is: do you want to take something off

Bray Wyatt has some words for the NXT Universe.

your network so people can watch it for free? There are a lot of people who say, 'I don't watch every pay-per-view on the Network, but I do watch NXT every week.' It's an hour show that you can watch whenever you want, and it's great for the Network. It makes a lot of people attached to the Network because it's consistent programming. NXT is counter, and I know that by being counter, the shine will eventually wear off. But right now, we're new, we're exciting, we're different. We need to deliver a consistently good product so the WWE Universe stays consistently engaged. That's the challenge, but it's also what I love about it.

"The charm of what we do is partly based on it being counter to what WWE is. WWE is stadiums and massive arenas and pyro

Sami Zayn was the fifth NXT Champion in history.

Becky Lynch embraces Sasha Banks and Bayley at *NXT Takeover: Brooklyn*.

assaulting your senses. NXT is about the in-ring product. It doesn't matter if we have 13,000 people in there if they're not loud. We have 500 people at our shows and they're going crazy. It's awesome that we could sell 13,000 tickets, but it's a bit bothersome to run a show that big because it's not the intimate type of show that fans love. As long as we're doing that only a couple of times a year, I'm okay with it. WWE won't run a stadium every day because it's not good for business.

"You rent a stadium once a year for *WrestleMania* and it's awesome; we have 90,000 people and it's amazing. For us, that stadium is 13,000 people. I want to keep NXT what it is. NXT is intimate. When we run a 1,500-seat venue, and it's electric. The larger you go, the more of that personal feeling you lose. Same holds true for music. I've seen Metallica play in a stadium, I've seen Metallica play in an arena, and I've also sat in a room and watched them jam with nobody else there except for my wife. That was the ultimate thing I've ever seen them do. It was intimate. It was special. If I saw them play in a club, I'd feel the same way. There's something magical about being in those small venues. It's raw and it's gritty and it's what the brand is. I'm being pressured massively to add pyro in our show. I'm not doing pyro in there. We're not a pyro brand. We're not rockets and kaboom; we're ding-ding-ding and two guys wrestle. That's what we're all about. I don't want NXT to be about special effects. I don't want it to be about the size of the video wall. Finn Bálor's entrance isn't about special effects, his entrance is about cool. That's what I like about it. So I try to make 13,000 seats feel intimate because I like intimate. I like giving you the feeling that this is your brand and that you're a part of it. You're not just one of a bazillion people watching.

"NXT is *you*. NXT is your thing. And that's what keeps people watching and coming back for more. Fans are engaged because they're cheering for the stars they helped create. If you were a fan when Charlotte had her first match on TV, and then you watched when Charlotte fought for the Championship for the first time, and you went so crazy because you helped create the Divas Revolution, you feel like you helped create something special. You were there for the NXT Women who tore down the house while the *Raw* Divas got five minutes a match, and you were on Twitter with the hashtag #GiveDivasAChance. I want fans to feel like this movement is theirs because then they engage with these characters. Ten years from now, they'll still be talking about how they saw Charlotte in her very first match. They're not only connected to the movement, they helped create it.

"And NXT isn't only about the future of WWE; you can argue that it's the hottest thing in the entire industry right now . . . and we're only getting started."